Sip W9-AFL-473

A VOW OF
CONVERSATION

BOOKS BY THOMAS MERTON

The Asian Journal
Bread in the Wilderness
Conjectures of a Guilty Bystander
Contemplation in a World of Action
Disputed Questions
Gandhi on Non-Violence
The Hidden Ground of Love (Letters, Vol. I)
Ishi Means Man
Life and Holiness
The Literary Essays of Thomas Merton
The Living Bread
Love and Living
The Monastic Journey
My Argument with the Gestapo
Mystics and Zen Masters
The New Man
New Seeds of Contemplation
No Man Is an Island
The Nonviolent Alternative
Seasons of Celebration
The Secular Journal of Thomas Merton
Seeds of Destruction
The Seven Storey Mountain
The Sign of Jonas
The Silent Life
Thoughts in Solitude
The Waters of Siloe
Zen and the Birds of Appetite

POETRY

The Collected Poems of Thomas Merton
Emblems of a Season of Fury
The Strange Islands
Selected Poems
The Tears of the Blind Lions

TRANSLATIONS

Clement of Alexandria
The Way of Chuang Tzu
The Wisdom of the Desert

THOMAS MERTON

A Vow of Conversation

JOURNALS 1964–1965

Edited and with a Preface by
NAOMI BURTON STONE

FARRAR · STRAUS · GIROUX
NEW YORK

Copyright © 1988 by the Merton Legacy Trust
Preface copyright © 1988 Naomi Burton Stone
All rights reserved
First edition, 1988
Printed in the United States of America
Published simultaneously in Canada by Collins Publishers, Toronto
Designed by Jack Harrison

Library of Congress Cataloging-in-Publication Data
Merton, Thomas, 1915–1968.
  A vow of conversation.
    1. Merton, Thomas, 1915–1968—Diaries. 2. Trappists—United States—
Diaries. 3. Monks—United States—Diaries. I. Stone, Naomi Burton. II. Title.
BX4705.M542A3   1988b   271'.125024 [B]   88-3981

PREFACE
by Naomi Burton Stone

At first it seemed as if all that were needed to introduce the background of *A Vow of Conversation* would be a few quotations from the correspondence between Thomas Merton and me in 1968. But the more I looked at the relevant passages in our letters of that year, the more I was convinced that out-of-context pieces of letters do not really tell the whole story. I had to keep reminding myself that while *Vow* is a writer's Journals of 1964–65, edited by its author, our correspondence about it was written, and the actual work of editing took place, three years later, in 1968, at a time when Tom was living full-time in his hermitage. I was then living in Maine, working as a part-time editor at Doubleday, with a brief visit each month to New York City. I was also acting as Tom's unofficial literary adviser, with the knowledge and approval of the Abbot of Gethsemani and of my publishing employers.

I had first heard of *Vow* in a letter dated February 13, 1968, in which Tom wrote: "Within another couple of months I hope to send you the text of the Journal I have been keeping lately, years 1964 and '65 to be exact. Title: *A Vow of Conversation*. But I don't want to rush into print with it. Others before this, if possible."

There were plenty of other manuscripts by him to choose from— in fact, an unprecedented number of collections, projects, and suggestions. There was the pre-monastic novel, *Journal of My Escape from the Nazis*, finally called *My Argument with the Gestapo*, which I had admired but failed to sell to any publisher in the early 1940s. I was anxious to see it published and Doubleday brought it out in 1969. Four other items were also mentioned—a "collection of literary essays"; a long and fascinating piece on the Cargo movement, which Tom saw as part of a collection of similar or compatible articles, perhaps to be called *Prophets and Primitives*, but which Doubleday saw as part of a whole book devoted to Cargo, which had absolutely nothing to do with the ideas in Tom's head; essays on monasticism in the 1960s, which were published posthumously by Doubleday under the title *Contemplation in a World of Action*, edited by Br. Patrick Hart, O.C.S.O.; and "the love essays," later to become the Farrar, Straus and Giroux book *Love and Living*.

In our correspondence at this time there were enough references to this new Journal book to make me realize it was important, even though *My Argument with the Gestapo* became the chief subject of our letters because it had run into weighty editorial opposition at Doubleday, which took time to resolve.

On February 28, 1968, Tom wrote: "*Vow of Conversation* will be along in say two months (counting the amount of time it takes to get anything retyped . . .)." He seemed to have dropped the "A" from the title, perhaps victim to the frequent use of compression and abbreviation in his letters; at any rate, I don't appear to have mentioned its absence. The original title, as given in his first letter, is being retained.

On March 3, 1968, Tom wrote: "More I think of the other, *Vow of Conversation*, the more I see it will have to be held up, because it gives too many details about the hermitage and so on. Problem is that people come here and find their way to it. And more and more people come. I've been chasing them out. Lately too, one mystical (?) lady appeared on the scene. Quite a sane-seeming girl, but with a whole new lowdown on the Apocalypse and a whole new program for *me*, if you please. It looks as if she is going to be a problem, but she has not thank God come up here yet. Only to the gatehouse. If I need a refuge, can I escape to Maine and stay with you and Ned?"

On July 20, 1968, the manuscript of *Vow* was mailed to me in

Maine with a covering letter from Tom which said: "I went through it and it reads all right, though it strikes me as rather slight. Still, it will fit in as a sequel to all the others [i.e., Journals] of the same nature, and there will be some who will enjoy it. The only problem as far as I can see is the timing. I certainly don't want it printed before 1971. As to editing, of course it will need a lot. There are passages about Dom James that lack perspective and perhaps charity, though I was only telling the truth. However . . . Well, you have a blue pencil. They do fit into a little sort of story. The one thing I am definite about is putting the book off for a while."

On July 24 I wrote, among other matters, to acknowledge *Vow*: "Thanks too for the Journal. I will read it as soon as I can. The summer is absolutely wild. It's not just the darling grandchildren and so on, but the fact that all authors finish their books at this season and expect instant answers. So I am piled high, and since we are talking of 1971 publication . . ."

On August 19, 1968, in a letter about *My Argument*, Tom adds: "As to *Vow of Conversation*, I just wanted to get it on paper. There is no sweat about getting it in print, or even read by my editor." On August 27, announcing the pending arrival of a collection of literary essays, which he would appreciate my looking over, he says: "I think *Vow of Conversation* is more slight than *Conjectures* [*of a Guilty Bystander*] but still passable—in 1971. Have you looked at it yet?"

On September 2, 1968, I finally wrote a two-page omnibus letter in which I said: "I started reading *Vow of Silence* [sic] and am crazy about it. I am not gulping it down more than I can help, but it is very hard to stop reading it. It seems to me the most mature writing you have done. I believe you have learned to complain without bitterness, and I feel much greater understanding of what has been eating you. Also this kind of writing seems to me to have a much greater message for ordinary people, and it's a feast of ideas and insights into contemporary and non-contemporary thought and writing. Wonderful. I suppose there are a few hacks at your brothers here and there, but they didn't seem to me out of place at all and needed to be said. One feels, actually, that you are using restraint. I hate to wait till 1971, but so be it."

My letter ended: "More later when I have finished *Vow of Silence*

[sic]. But please be assured that I think it great and don't agree at all that it is a lesser book than *Conjectures*." Tom knew that *Conjectures* was my favorite book.

It is painful to read over these letters, which turned out to be among the last I received from Tom. It is a measure of his kindness that he never reproved me, even though I disregarded every canon of good editorial practice when I finally did get around to writing him. Literary agents and editors are not supposed to *have* grandchildren or any other excuse for being appalling correspondents. Much worse than that, they should *never* refer to other authors or their manuscripts. The author to whom one is writing or speaking is the Only One. Finally, I did the unforgivable—I misquoted his title, not once but twice. Yet Tom's reply never mentioned this. Anyone looking for evidence in his life of heroic sanctity would have to put this restraint high on the list.

Tom's letter of September 6 is a long one, much of it given to the exciting and joyful news that in a few days he would be leaving for a meeting of the abbots of all Catholic monastic orders in Asia. There would also be an interfaith meeting in India and visits to other Trappist monasteries in Asia. He said:

I'm so glad you like *Vow of Conversation*. It makes me feel better about it. Still, it has one big problem attached. Life where I am now in this hermitage will be hardly livable after it is published. Already people are finding it and barging in, and if they read so many details about it they might as well come in Cook's Tours. Another thing, too, is that it is awfully what the new-look crowd calls subjective, introspective, etc. I know there's nothing wrong with that, but this particular book will, I know, come in for some awful whacks from the Catholic press. Which reminds me: what I meant about the liturgical conference was not just guitar Masses or such. You don't seem to realize it ended up as a sort of wild party, priest and nuns necking all over the Sheraton Whatsis, a masked ball affair with priests dressed up as clowns (and well they might). At least that's what I got out of it all. Maybe the reports were a bit slanted. The point is that this viewpoint is so vociferous now and so utterly intolerant that one has to be a little careful. I don't like to see a book as personal as this simply ridiculed by all these loud asses. Lack of humility?

Must stop now. My feeling is that perhaps the next book after *Gestapo*

PREFACE

should be the *Monastic Essays*, which are controversial but still I think can stand up on their own merits against the extremist view, and hence present no problem. Also, they might get out of date if we wait four or five years. Naturally, I'll have to do some work on them when I get back. We could then consider whether *Lit.[erary] Essays* or *Vow of Conversation* would be next, but in any case that would bring us to 1971. (*Gestapo* '69, *Mon. Essays* '70.)

Do please pray that this journey may mean all that I hope it will mean, and more. I know it may seem a bit wild, running around like this, but I do think it is absolutely important and necessary both for me, for the Church, and for the Asian religions which are not yet in the same kind of crisis we are, but will be.

All my very best. Blessings, prayers, affection, peace in the Lord,

Tom.

In his letter of July 20, 1968, Tom said this book would need a lot of editing, and indicated that I might do it. But editing has always seemed to me a matter of suggestion rather than the arbitrary use of a blue pencil. It is true that there are "uncharitable" remarks in this book, but they didn't seem to me very serious in 1968 and seem less so today. If the text of this book had been taken from a currently kept Journal, with little time for the author to revise it, and presented hot off the stove of frustration, severe editing would perhaps have been justified. But it was prepared and edited by Thomas Merton himself from material written three years earlier. In 1968 he himself recognized a possible lack of perspective and charity, but let certain remarks stand. While the book has been copyedited professionally, my editing has been aimed solely at being faithful to the original and at leaving the text alone.

One reason why I am comfortable with not deleting a few remarks that "lack perspective" is this: for the most part they concern Dom James, the Abbot of Gethsemani for so many years, who died on Good Friday in 1987 at the age of ninety-one. Ever since we met in 1949, when I first visited Gethsemani, Dom James and I were good friends. I am sure, from many talks with him about Tom and from the letters we exchanged, that nothing in this book would have been a big surprise to Dom James, or unduly painful. He knew Tom, loved and admired him. Years ago I advocated publishing this book, because there had been too much speculation as to why it had not been published long before. It seemed clear to me from his reference to 1971 that the kind of delay Tom had in mind was two or three years, not fifteen or twenty. That is why I offered to take up this matter with Dom James, but I lost that round. Instead, the original typescript was made available to some selected scholars and writers, to be read without any note-taking. This resulted in less than accurate quotation and in the end caused Dom James considerable pain. But not, incidentally, any animosity toward Tom.

Looking back to the time when Tom's letter of July 20, 1968, was written, it occurs to me that the mention of "lack of perspective and perhaps charity" might have been a defense mechanism at work. Tom did not altogether appreciate my friendship with Dom James, and we often argued about it. If he admitted in advance the book needed editing, then perhaps he thought I would not be pained and shocked and tiresome, as I often was. When I finally wrote him about the book with enthusiasm, he dropped the charitable-editing suggestion. I am sure that Tom did have very real feelings about making changes in the book of such a character that everyone who drove by Gethsemani would not feel free to drop in on the hermit for a chat. But I believe that his stated feelings regarding the reception of this book by the Roman Catholic avantgarde of the sixties may have been the real reason he wanted the book held up for a while.

It is necessary to remember the sixties, a period of so much turmoil, with the pendulum swinging from Trent to Vatican II and in some cases far beyond (and alas far far behind) the sense and import of the Council documents. Tom had been for years in the vanguard of the Peace Movement, had supported racial justice with his heart and his pen, had been a leader in monastic renewal, so it may seem odd that he was so critical of the liturgical conference of clowns, for example. It is not odd, really. He was so far ahead of us in the real life of prayer and silence that he understandably didn't want *A Vow of Conversation* trodden on because it might be judged superficially and found wanting in an era and atmosphere of heady excesses that he knew would pass. At the same time I don't think he envisaged quite so long a delay.

A word about the title. There's no doubt that the title of this book is a play on words. Cistercian monks take five vows—poverty, chastity, obedience, stability, and conversion of manners (*conversatio morum*). In *The Sign of Jonas* Merton writes of a discussion he had in 1947 with Dom Dominique, the Abbot General of the Cistercians: "Dom Dominique said that sanctity, for a Cistercian, consisted in allowing oneself to be formed through obedience. He also said that our vow of conversion of manners amounted, in practice, to a vow to do always what is more perfect. That is not altogether easy."

In the period covered by this book, 1964–65, while he was still novice master at the abbey, Tom was allowed to live part-time in his hermitage, spending not only days but some nights there. He was also given permission to receive groups of visitors, and even to make one visit to New York City to meet with Dr. D.T. Suzuki. He was steadily moving toward the life of a full-time hermit, which I believe he saw as "what is more perfect." The hermit who stays in his abode and receives visitors is definitely in the tradition, and given also this particular hermit's gift for communication, *A Vow of Conversation* seems to me an ironic summing-up of this period of Tom's life.

1964

January 1, 1964

Yesterday the year drew to a quiet curious end with an eclipse of the moon. The novices and I went out into the fierce zero cold and stood in the darkness of the garden while a last flake of light resisted for a long time the swallowing globe of dark. Then I went back to read Karl Jasper's book about Plato.

We have a Japanese fish kite made of red paper and Brother Dunstan stuck up some bamboo poles in the Zen garden. We will fly fish and streamers to celebrate the New Year.

The year of the dragon came in with sleet crackling on all the quiet windows. The year of the hare went out yesterday with our red fish kite twisting and flopping in the wind over the Zen garden. Today, a cold gray afternoon. Much snow. Woods, bright with snow, loom out of the dark. Totally new vision of the Vineyard Knob. Dark, etched out with snow, standing in obscurity and in a kind of strange spaciousness that I had never observed before.

The wide sweep of snow on St. Benedict's field. I climbed the Lake Knob. Wonderful woods. Slid down the steep hillside in the snow. Tore my pants on barbed wire. Came back through the vast fields and drifts of snow. Peace!

*   *   *

Bultmann's idea of God. I write this in the evening before the night watch. Bultmann says our care meets God at the end of its capacity where He limits our care and cuts it short. Our love of beauty, our need for love, our desire to work—Bultmann's God is the power who limits all this, who sets a terminus to all this. From Bultmann's essays: "It is God who makes man finite, who makes a comedy of man's care, who allows his longings to miscarry, who casts him into solitude, who sets a terminus to his knowing . . . Yet at the same time it is God who forces man into life and drives him into care."

Curious? But it is a Biblical notion of God and very real.

Another quote from Bultmann: "Real belief in God always grows out of the realization that being is an unknown quantity which cannot be learned and retained in the form of a proposition but which one is always becoming conscious of in the moment of living."

*   *   *

Let me therefore inscribe this at the head of a New Year, not of the dragon but of the Lord:

> If in Christian belief in God, we understand the claims of the moment to be those of the Thou and of the demand to love, then it is clear that its crisis is in the constant struggle of hate against love and that this crisis becomes acute in every encounter with the Thou which thoughtlessly or selfishly we would disregard, maintaining our own rights, our own interest in contempt or in undisguised hate. (Bultmann)

January 3

Warm wind. Bright sun. Melting snow. Water off the roof splashing in all the buckets around the hermitage. A good letter from Ernesto Cardenal came today. He has been staying with the Cuna Indians on the San Blas Islands off Panama and he speaks very highly of them, loves them very much. Says that they have been pacifists for hundreds of years. It is a wonder they still survive.

Heidegger has the notion that the realization and acceptance of death is the guarantee of authenticity in life and existence. This is rather close to Rancé and probably a better formulation of what the Abbot of La Grande Trappe himself saw and wanted to say. It is in short a very monastic intuition and I find much in the existentialists that is monastic.

In any case, Heidegger is also fully Socratic. For instance, in his idea of "nothing." "Knowledge is, in its very validity, a form of untruth because it conceals the ignorance which it does not abolish" (Blackham, *Six Existentialist Thinkers*).

January 4

I got a letter from Jean Héring this morning. He is still in Strasbourg, retired, living in the old city. It was a very good letter and he sent some bibliographical references. I want to look up some of his early articles. (This is a Protestant professor of theology with whom I stayed in Strasbourg when I was a student in the 1930s.)

* * *

A hunter, a fat-bottomed Robin Hood in a green outfit, was blasting into the treetops up at the end of my field to the east of the hermitage, too far for an edifying shout—but he went away on his own.

* * *

The French nuclear deterrent shows something of the ridiculousness of this theory of war.

One, it can never really protect France against a serious determination on the part of an enemy to destroy it. It can only make the enemy "pay for it" and think twice, consequently, before wiping France out.

Two, the payment? Cities, cities only. There is no intention whatever of counterforce strategy, not even a pretense. Such a strategy would be totally useless. Not that the destruction of cities would be useful. This is the tactic of "the elder daughter of the Church" in the land of Saint Louis. It is possible St. Bernard would have approved. Our late Abbot General certainly did.

Three, if missiles are used, the country may have five minutes' warning. That is to say, it will take the missiles of the enemy five minutes to arrive. Nothing is said about how long it will take the computer to figure out whether or not they are missiles.

Four, planes will take fifteen minutes from Russia, but how to identify them? Five, the decision will be determined by computers. Machines will decide whether Christian France is menaced and ought to wipe out a few Russian cities.

It is taken as an article of Christian faith that the menace will come from Russia. This does not seem to be questioned even for a moment.

Five minutes in which to ask questions. Who will think of a good one? At any rate, only the machine can answer and probably only the machine can ask the question.

January 6, Epiphany

Bultmann's essays are very revealing. Every sentence tends to stop me and I don't seem to get anywhere. I am snowed under by it. The extraordinary grasp of Greek thought he has and which he always transcends in order to end in a Biblical and eschatological freedom. The seminal influence of Heidegger, whom he appropriates and develops in a fully New Testament and kerygmatic way. It is fantastically good. How many of my own old ideas I can now abandon or revise!

He has made clear to me the full limitations of all my early work, which is too naïve, insufficient except in what concerns my own experience. He says, "Grace can never be possessed but can only be received afresh again and again." "Man comes into his present situation as in some way under constraint, so that real freedom can only be received as a gift."

One of the great temptations of an over-institutionalized religion is precisely this: to keep man under the constraint of his own and his society's past, so that this safety appears to be freedom. He is "free" to return to the familiar constraint but this interferes with his freedom to respond to the new gift of grace in Christ. This raises the whole problem of outward forms of worship, etc., and I think that Bultmann is so far weak in his concept of the Church. But this is nevertheless a great truth which must be brought into our view of the Church. Otherwise, where is the Holy Spirit? Where is the soul of this body?

The dread of being oneself is the great obstacle to freedom, for freedom equals being oneself and acting accordingly. The flight to an external authority for approval. Contrary to that: ability to make decisions as though they were not subject to the comment of other men. True solitude! Solitude of the poet in his decisions. Bultmann has a very real notion of tradition. Not a past in which to find a refuge. "True loyalty to tradition does not consist in the canonization of a particular stage in history . . . always criticism of the present before the tribunal of tradition but also criticism of tradition before the tribunal of the present day. *Real loyalty does not involve repetition but carrying things a stage further,*" and "Freedom from the past does not result in the denial of the past but in the positive appreciation of it."

January 7
Thick, curious icy mist. Vile weather for a cold, which I have. The mist has made a wonderful abstract pigment out of the silvery mass of manure in the night pasture. The dry weeds, too, are silver with it.

*   *   *

Pope Paul has visited Palestine. Many curious symbolic happenings as he visited the holy places. After landing in Jordan and driving to Jerusalem, he tried to make the Via Crucis. First he was met by people with palm branches, "recalling Christ's triumphal entrance into Jerusalem," said the United Press man. Then there were women veiled in black on the housetops clapping rhythmically. Then the crowd of one hundred thousand got out of control. Not hostile, not friendly, just out of control. All rushing at the Pope. Some with reason, some without, some shouting in Arabic, "The father, the father."
Then, says the press, the crowd became "hysterical."
The Pope was rushed through the first Stations of the Cross without being able to see them, let alone stop and pray. At the station of Veronica's veil, he took refuge in the entry of a convent and "his face was ashen."
He finally got to the Basilica of the Holy Sepulchre. A TV cable over his head caught fire while he was trying to say Mass. All the lights were out most of the time of his Mass.
The whole narrative of this first day or so was of the Pope being

hustled by huge crowds, carried through mobs by Arab policemen or having a way beaten for him by clubs.

As I was leaving the refectory early, I heard something read about his plan to go by car to Nazareth, meeting high Israeli officials at Megiddo, "the Biblical Armageddon."

The whole story had a strange ominous sound about it. It seemed fraught with a symbolic seriousness which I could not interpret or fathom in any way. As if something urgent were being announced and something else even more strange. Perhaps the momentary disappearance of the Church in a huge whirlpool of confusion caused by masses of people milling around. Coming on top of the mass trauma following Kennedy's assassination, with the explicit foreboding that the Pope himself might be murdered, this news item gives the impression that the world is slowly going completely mad. And no solemnity, no gesture of servility, pleasantness, or good will can prevent the unknown fury that is breaking without explanation.

*   *   *

I got a good note from Father Placide at Bellefontaine, thanking me for my card which complimented him on his draft of the new directory for the monastic life. He said there were quite a few objections from Dutch abbots that it was too traditional and from American abbots that it was too favorable to the hermit life. The book has never been published. This was one of the best books produced by anyone in our order on the monastic life for a long time. Significant that it could not arrive at publication.

January 10
Ad Reinhardt has sent all kinds of fine paper, especially some thin—almost transparent—Japanese sheets on which I have found a way of crudely printing abstract calligraphies which in some cases turn out exciting, at least to me.

*   *   *

A fine afternoon after yesterday's rain. The snow has been washed away. The hills are purple and cold, sharply outlined.

8

*   *   *

Dom James left today for Rome. Three of us separately had told him he might become Abbot General. I, Father Prior (Flavian) and Father Eudes. Apparently this worried him enough to keep him awake last night.

*   *   *

Half the community seem to be making up new liturgical offices, reorganizing the liturgy, planning new ways of prayer. After a thousand years of inertia, it is now every man for himself.

The Pope's short visit to Palestine and his talk with Patriarch Athenagoras seem to have been after all something quite magnificent. A great thing. A sign of real life full of hope and meaning and yet with certain ambiguities remaining.

*   *   *

Father H. A. Reinhold has given my manuscript on "Peace in the Post-Christian Era" to Bishop Wright, who apparently is reading it with interest and seems to like it. What if he took it with him to the next Council session? I don't know.

January 11

I am moved by Father David Kirk's notes on Patriarch Maximos of Antioch. Obviously one of the greatest men in the Church today. He is doing a lot for the monastic life.

*   *   *

Much as I disagree with some of Bultmann's statements on non-Christian religion, I cannot help being swayed and moved by his basic argument, which is completely convincing and most salutary. "God's grace is to man grace in such a thoroughgoing sense that it supports the whole of man's existence, and can only be conceived of as grace by those who surrender their whole existence and let themselves fall into the unfathomable dizzy depths without seeking for something to hold on to."

The great hope of our time is, it seems to me, not that the

Church will become once again a world power, a dominant institution, but on the contrary, that the power of faith and spirit will shake the world when Christians have lost what they held on to and have entered into the eschatological kingdom. That is where, in fact, they already are. But they do not know how to let go and fall into the depths where there is nothing to hold on to. They do not trust God to shake the world: they prefer to shake it themselves. This means their own ruin. He shakes it, after all!

*   *   *

From a certain point of view, my monastic life does bring me "close to God" but this closeness is an illusion unless I see it also in some sense as conflict with God and therefore as dread.

Monastic peace or monastic dread? Both. The monastic life as "a sure thing," as an answer to every problem, can become a great illusion and prevarication, almost the denial of the essence of Christianity.

*   *   *

Bultmann, again: "It is not just what is transitory in man that is given over to death, not just what is subject to fate, so that his will to live now triumphs and his old ego is perpetuated in his indomitable will to live. On the contrary, man is given over to death in his entirety, so that he has become a new man in a radical sense. But that means that his will has become a new will and that in the security of his possession of immortality he is not relieved of all claims and he cannot enjoy his new life with a mind set at rest."

*   *   *

Blackham, writing of Sartre, says wisely that popular wisdom easily accepts *extreme* views but not *disturbing* ones. The extreme view that to live well is impossible, or the other extreme that to live well is easy: this they will readily accept. But Sartre's claim that to live well is difficult and possible, they reject as despair.

Sartre's courage is laudable. His stoicism is insufficient. His seriousness is the kind that makes possible the conflict and contact described by Bultmann. In this I praise him.

10

But his dogmatic humanism has no point except as a useful illusion.

January 13

Yesterday it snowed and there was sleet, wind and cold. Clear frozen surface on the new snow. Sleet like the manna in Exodus, but useless, and after I had plowed my way around among the pine trees in a walk before Vespers, with snow flying into my eyes, my neck began to hurt.

Saturday was a bright day, even warm. Victor and Carolyn Hammer came over from Lexington.

Saturday evening I got a call from Monsignor McCormack in New York. He was down here a month ago to get me to write a short script for a movie in the Vatican Pavilion at the New York World's Fair. I did and it was mostly about charity, peace, racial justice, etc. Now he calls and evidently the text has been to Spellman and back in the meantime. The indications are that all this must be replaced by an apologetic textbook piece on the Church as the one true Church. What we have that is different from the Protestants and Orthodox. To dispel any confusion that may have been created by all this ecumenical business!

I suppose this was to have been expected. I asked him to send down notes of what he wants and I will try to write them up. I am a bit doubtful about getting anything worthwhile out of this. Perhaps a few lines that will have meaning for someone outside the Church. The rest: will it even support Catholics in their convictions or just be another four minutes of familiar jargon?

*　　*　　*

Jaspers talks of the Augustinian turnabout. At one moment Augustine is saying, "Let none of us say that he has already found the truth, let us look for it as though we did not already know it from either side." And later he advocates using force against those who do not accept our faith, apparently without feeling there is any problem or contradiction! As the greatest of Roman Catholic doctors, he has bequeathed this mentality to the entire Catholic Church, and to the Protestants as well, because he is as much their father as ours. This turnaround is then deep in the mind of Western Christendom.

*   *   *

If, in my Vatican Pavilion movie script, I give the impression of openness and persuasion, will this not be a deception? Will I not simply be standing up as a front for those who want to use force or moral pressure on non-Catholics? The temptation is to deliberately write a closed, impassive, inattentive series of declarations and let the heathens draw their own conclusions from my cool approach! But you cannot yet fully count on people reading between the lines.

January 14

I learned this morning of the death of Paul Hindemith. It is about ten years since his visit here. I remember he and I and his wife took a long walk through the woods at the foot of Vineyard Knob and talked about many things. He had just directed the first performance of *The Harmony of the World* in Minneapolis. He was talking about his collaboration with Brecht, which was very funny, and about the "Ite angeli veloces" of Claudel. He was a great person. I have not heard half of what he has written.

*   *   *

It is zero weather. The novitiate thermometer, which is quite conservative, registered ten above, but others were claiming that their thermometers were ten below. The snow is deep. It sparkles in the sun under the trees.

I wrote a few final pages for *Art and Worship* on the Council Constitution and also a preface.

January 16

5:10 a.m. At Cîteaux it is noon. We may already have a new Abbot General and may learn his name even before the conventual Mass of the Holy Spirit is sung to implore grace for the election.

*   *   *

Some notes that come to mind in connection with Merleau-Ponty: When men speak, we assume they have something to say and know what it is. How often are these assumptions well founded?

Ambiguity of man, who tries to emerge from his own darkness and yet wants not to emerge.

How often is speech an excuse for remaining incommunicado on the grounds that one has "communicated," one has done his duty?

The artist who recognizes and loves his own style to the great damage of his work, the style being imagined as himself. At this point he begins to know and will his style, as it were, without contact with the world outside, whereas, in reality, the style is only a by-product of that contact. Thus, you get style without contact, style without communication which is nevertheless accepted as communication.

Then it becomes necessary in such a situation to write anti-poetry. For what appears to be poetry and what appears to be communication is actually a common plot to repudiate poetry and refuse communication. The pretense has to be attacked with the anti-poem. The anti-poem is positive communication of resistance against the sham rituals of conventional communication.

Emblems: equivalences. Finding my own system of emblems. A picture of the back of Braque's white head, surrounded by his own bird emblems. He looks at you sitting in a corduroy jacket. (Braque is dead.)

Finding figures of being, or seeming to, when the painter no longer seems to himself to find these. He is dead. That is, he does not encounter the world, for the figure is his encounter.

Response to the past. One's own previous work, the work of others, renewing the life that was in them.

I have an obligation to Paul Klee which goes deeper, even into the order of theology. An obligation about which I have done nothing. Knowing he is there in some museums or in the Skira [art] books is not enough. Nor is mimicry. My obligation is to seriously question him and reply to his question addressed to me, to justify in some sense the faith in me which he never knew he had (or how would he know *me*?). But he painted me, nevertheless, whether he wanted to or not.

The artist has not been demonstrated to be a failure because of his memories appearing in his work. He may have succeeded in using all his experiences, even his sickness, to interpret the world.

January 17

St. Anthony's Feast. Yesterday at the beginning of the afternoon work, as I was settling down to change a typewriter ribbon and rewrite the script for the Vatican Pavilion, Brother Dennis came and told me that Dom Ignace Gillet, Abbot of Aiguebelle, was the new Abbot General. Later Brother Dennis wanted to know if I thought the new General was a "return to sources" man and I said I did not know.

*   *   *

For Merleau-Ponty, our body is not an apparatus which, directed by the spirit, makes use of pre-existing signs to express a meaning which is there. It is on the contrary, a living instrument of its one life, making *sense* by all its acts, making sense of the world in which it is. The whole body is art and full of art. Corporeity is style. A deeply (religious) spiritual concept. Corporeity—a sense and focus of intelligent convergences.

"Le propre du geste humain . . . *d'imaginer un sens*" (*Signes*, p. 85).

All gestures, part of a universal syntax, the projection of monograms and inscapes. History as "horizontal transcendence" becomes a sacred cow. That is to say, an external power bearing down on us inexorably and demanding the immolation of the present, the recognition of our nothingness in the present of what "man will one day be" (for as yet he is not).

*   *   *

Merleau-Ponty sees, more rightly than most Christians, that in fact Christianity *abolished* subordination and revealed a new mystery in the relation of man to God that is *not* vertical only or horizontal only, for Christ bears witness that God would not be fully God if he did not espouse the human condition. "In Christ we find God as our other self who dwells in our obscurity and makes it authentic," as Merleau-Ponty says.

14

The whole mystery of the Ascension is here. Why do you stand looking up into heaven? "Transcendence does not lean down on man and dominate. Man becomes strangely the privileged carrier of transcendence."

Stalinist and Marxist history becomes a neurosis of the future. A non-philosophy. History—the judgment not of intentions only, nor of consequences only, but of the measure in which values have passed into facts by virtue of free action (Hegel). Hence, the maturation of the future in the present, not the sacrifice of the present to the future. This is a brilliant diagnosis of the wrong of our time—the dialectic between the pessimism of the neo-Marxist and the laziness of the non-Marxist in complicity with each other to produce the power of lies and frustration—*le puissance de mensonge et d'échec*—which stifles the whole world in self-deception and transforms everything into futility because it makes us blind to the "grace of the event" and strangles expression, therefore history. For history is language, i.e., dialogue in which the speakers (the artist, the politician and so forth) lead each other to new values which they can recognize as being their own. "The perpetual conversation which is pursued in and through all words and all valid actions."

January 18

I wonder if anyone still reads the monastic letters of Abelard. They are full of fine traditional material in the manner of Jerome. Clear, precise and among the best monastic writings of the twelfth century. I am reading them now and using them in the course I am giving on St. Bernard, in connection with Bernard's *De Conversione*. I ought to do an article on Abelard's monastic letters but I don't have time. I have been unable to buy Schmitt's edition of Anselm. We have two volumes on interlibrary loan from West Baden. I have them until Easter and want to work on some of Anselm's letters too.

*   *   *

The great impact of Walker Percy's novel, *The Moviegoer*, is that the whole book says in reality what the hero is not, and expresses his existential awareness of what he is not. His sense of alienation, his comparative refusal to be alienated as everybody else is (not successful), his comparative acceptance of this ambiguity and failure. This is a book full of emblems and patterns of light (the misty place where they fish, or, rather, his mother fishes, is like a vague movie too).

Merleau-Ponty says: "The novelist converses with his reader in a *language of initiates*: people initiated into the universe of possibilities contained in the human body" (*Signes*, p. 95). This describes exactly the awareness that is so consistently alive in Walker Percy's book. See the scene with the crippled child. "What *we want to say* is not right in front of us outside of every word as a pure significance. It is only the excess of what we live over what has already been said." Merleau-Ponty (*Signes*, p. 104).

Authentic expression equals a spontaneous elucidation of what we do not yet realize, rather than a final statement of what we have acquired as knowledge. But we tend to look at it the other way round. We pretend to say "what we know." Our genuine "surplus" is what we do not yet know, and what will come to be known in our saying it to someone who will reply. For instance, I am not now saying something I alone know, but what I have not fully comprehended in Merleau-Ponty and what he did not know because it is my response and what will (or will not) be elucidated in the response of some other. (Yet the author does not need to be aware of the reader whose response fulfills his meaning.) If this further response is merely "objective," it is as yet nothing and it is as if I too had said nothing. But I don't mind. Someone else may hear what is here. It is not my business to determine *who* will respond or *how*. I say my own word and pass on.

January 19

Last night I dreamed I was speaking to a kind and friendly Benedictine and saying to him with confident happiness and abandon that I *deserved* punishment for my sins, that I deserved it and accepted it gladly. He was apparently deprecating this as if it were "too extreme" a spirituality, and yet as though at the same time he half admitted I was right. Then this morning in St. Anselm's meditations, I found his second meditation on the worthiness of doing penance. *Digne, certes, digne!*

Anselm's meditations and prayers are musical compositions. He can use his themes without inhibition, themes in which we others are now condemned to be inarticulate. For if we tried to say what he says, we could not be authentic today. Those forms have been worn out by tired monks. They no longer say what Anselm wanted them to say. Yet, how close he comes to existentialist nausea. For instance, in prayer 8 on St. John the Baptist. Yet there is always the hope, the presence of the compassionate Christ which is not permitted to the existentialist. I love Anselm. I love these prayers, though I could never attempt to use such language myself.

January 20

Importance of that solitude which is a solitary, spiritual, material, rehabilitation of the sensible. The sensible around me becoming conscious of itself in and through me. A solitude in which one allows nature this virginal silence, this secret, pure, unrelatable consciousness in oneself. The reality "before all thesis," before the beginning of dialectic and En-Soi. The singular and timeless (not part of any series) mutual exploration of silences and meanings with which my consciousness never manages to be quite simultaneous but in which my body is present. The self-awareness of the great present in which my body is fully and uniquely situated. "My" body? Not as "had" by me!

January 23

The retreat (which is now going on) brings up again the problem of my resentments, my frustrations, my sense of being unjustly treated, cheated in fact, to some extent exploited. There may be, from a certain point of view, some truth in this but if I attempt to treat others as guilty or to see in them indications of perverseness and failure of which they themselves can only be unconscious, it does no good to anyone. I have no need to judge and no capacity to.

What matters is the struggle to make the right adjustment in my own life and this upsets me because there is no pattern for me to follow and I don't have either the courage or the insight to follow the Holy Spirit in all freedom. Hence, my fear and my guilt, my indecisiveness, my hesitations, my backtracking, my attempts to cover myself when wrong, etc. Actually, it is a matter of deciding what limited and concrete view to take so as to fulfill my actual duty to God and to my community and thus be the monk I am supposed to be. I need only seek truth, as I am personally called to do in my own situation. If I were more a man of love and spirit, more a man of God, I would have no problems. So my job is to advance with the difficulty of one who lacks love and yet seeks it, in the realization that I am not supposed to solve all my problems for myself. Nor am I supposed to be a man of God in the sense of "having no problem." One of the sources of futile struggle in the spiritual life is the assumption that one has to become a person without problems, which is, of course, impossible. And if a man is struggling to be without problems in his life, he is beating his head against a brick wall.

*   *   *

A good, fruitful, though slightly anguished meditation in the wood by St. Malachy's field. The paradise smell under the pines. The warm sun. The seat of branches.

*   *   *

I need to find my way out of a constructed solitude, which is actually the chief obstacle to the realization of true solitude in openness and inner subjectivity. False solitude is built on an artificially induced awareness of unrealized possibilities of relationship with others. One prefers to keep these possibilities unrealized. (Hence, false solitude is a short-circuit of love.)

January 25
The year of the dragon has so far distinguished itself by strong lusty winds. A great storm the other night. Some trees blew down in the woods near the hermitage, including one in the path on the way up. Pine cones and bits of branches are strewn all over the lawn and last night, too, there were strong winds fighting the side of the monastery building. I still hear them grumbling around outside like friendly beasts.

18

At 3:30 in the morning, the moon over the cold garden full of wind.

*   *   *

"The major trick or deception used by power is to persuade men that they are winning when they are losing." So says Merleau-Ponty in commenting on Machiavelli. He commends the honesty of Machiavelli, for admitting that social conflict is the basis of all power. Also that the prince (leader) must not become the prisoner of a virtuous image of himself that would obstruct action made necessary by a sudden new aspect of the struggle for power. "True, strength of soul is needed, since, in between the will to please and defiance, it is necessary to conceive a historic enterprise in which all can join."

On this historic magnanimity and altruism (everyone gets in on the power project) Merleau-Ponty bases his defense of Machiavelli as a realistic moralist. He claims he establishes a genuine relationship while the moralizing politician really remains aloof. The realist, on the other hand, like Machiavelli's prince is one who accepts distance but mediates through it and creates a relationship with his subjects. I do not know if I agree with this analysis of Machiavelli by Merleau-Ponty but it is certainly interesting and novel. It seems to point in a dangerous direction in which perhaps we are all going. The direction of the acceptance of power and the power struggle and conflict as the *only* basis for fully realistic political relationships, even in a Christian sense. Thus raising the question: Can there be a Christian politics?

*   *   *

I am aware of the need for constant self-revision and growth, leaving behind the renunciations of yesterday and yet in continuity with all my yesterdays. For to cling to the past is to lose one's continuity with the past, since this means clinging to what is no longer there.

My ideas are always changing, always moving around one center, and I am always seeing that center from somewhere else.

Hence, I will always be accused of inconsistency. But I will no longer be there to hear the accusation.

January 26

"What makes us afraid is our great freedom in face of the emptiness that has still to be filled" (Karl Jaspers).

And again, these concluding words from his arresting little pamphlet on the European spirit: "The philosophically serious European is faced today with the choice between opposed philosophical possibilities. Will he enter the limited field of fixed truth, which in the end has only to be obeyed, or will he go into the limitless open truth? . . . Will he win this perilous independence in perilous openness as in existential philosophy, the philosophy of communication in which the individual becomes himself on condition that others become themselves, in which there is no solitary peace but *constant dissatisfaction* and in which a man exposes his soul to suffering."

This is a very valid intuition for monastic community life also. The realization of these two things, that each individual monk, or each individual member of any Christian community, becomes himself only on condition that he functions with others to help them to become themselves. In this interaction there is no refuge in solitary tranquillity. One is exposed to constant dissatisfaction and suffering by the fact that this process is frustrating and *always incomplete.*

February 2

Once again the question of getting to grips with my reality, coordinating, incorporating in a living sequence all that I can reach to make relevant my presence on earth—a presence which is contingent and soon to end.

* * *

The religious depth of Ammonas, the perspicacity of Merleau-Ponty, even the tedious subtlety of Sartre, and always the Bible. Meetings of opposites, not carefully planned exclusions, not mere acceptance of the familiar. A life of clashes and discoveries, not a life of repetitions. Deep dread before God, and not trivial excitement.

* * *

One of the worst things I have ever done was that absurd enterprise of writing a text for the Vatican Pavilion film. It has nothing whatever to do with the reality of the "movies." I have done nothing to "make a (real) movie." I must learn to refuse these baits—and yet, how marvelous it would be to really and competently do a true movie.

Merleau-Ponty's essay on the films had important implications I think for the new liturgy. Liturgy as behavior or comportment? Supposing one translated the language of the film into liturgy. One might take a text of Merleau-Ponty where he spoke of the films and replace the word "movies" by the word "liturgy." Where he says the cinema addresses itself to our power of deciphering the world and so forth.

Let us read such a text: "Liturgy addresses itself to our power to decipher the world of men and coexist with them." This is either so right or so utterly wrong as to be stupid. To me it is obviously *right*. Liturgy is to be experienced and so is a film. Both the liturgy and the film are to be *experienced* rather than *thought* or *willed*. Experienced by the "presentation of conducts." "Not each conscience and the other conscience . . . but the conscience thrown into the world, submitted to the view of others and learning from others what it is." This needs interpretation because there is a danger of the Fascist application or a Soviet application of it. But in the right sense, it can be liturgy, or can it?

Both film and liturgy: "The engagement of a conscience in a body."

February 7

Cold wind, dark sky and sleet.

I emerge from the end of Sartre's long, involved meditation on Baudelaire like one coming out of darkness underground into daylight, with this last sentence: "The free choice that man makes of himself is absolutely identified with what one calls his destiny."

To the superficial observer this would seem to be just what Sartre's liberty does not mean. For those who think this liberty is arbitrary and subject to no restraint or limit, Sartre's portrait of Baudelaire is the most clinical and exact condemnation of a liberty that is misused, inauthentic and steeped in bad faith.

In fact, for Sartre, Baudelaire is guilty of the primal sin of forcing together En-Soi and Pour-Soi and willing their impossible union. This is original sin in a very pure sense, although Sartre never uses that term. For in Sartre's philosophy, if En-Soi and Pour-Soi could be identified, their union would be God, and for Sartre, the reason why he says there is no God is that these two cannot be identified. To seek to identify En-Soi and Pour-Soi in oneself is to seek to be God, i.e., what Sartre would call static essence or pure nature or subject as object for eternity. (Pure narcissism = or carrying off the final metaphysical trick of eating your cake and having it.)

What Sartre regards as the sterility of Baudelaire's life ("going into the future backwards") is never for a moment justified by the beauty of his poetry. I think Sartre is right in seeing the puerility and unreality of Baudelaire's supposed Catholicism. This is a very hard, honest and objective book. One has a difficult time not agreeing with it and generally I do, when I understand it. Yet it is tiresome in its sustained, insolently dogmatic intensity, not even broken into chapters, barely into paragraphs. Paragraphs go for several pages.

Existentialism and Zen are here at one in condemning pure subjectivity and self-contemplation, and I am with them too. What remains to be seen is how much of himself Sartre was analyzing in Baudelaire. A recent autobiographical piece of Sartre's may give the answer to this ("Les Mots"). What answer? That we are all to some extent alike in our failure to be free, but some start out more handicapped than others.

*   *   *

It is curious that I have received more good reactions to the article on the Shakers in the January *Jubilee* than to almost any such thing I have written. Also quite a few reactions, at least three or four, to the letter on "Ecclesiastical Baroque" in this week's *Commonweal*. These reactions were not all either favorable or intelligent. One woman thought that because I was against covering priests with lace, I was attacking women! You can't win.

*   *   *

3:15 p.m. Right on time the SAC plane flies low over the blue hills slowly, ponderously, yet lightly as a shark in water making the wide turn in relative quiet, pretending we are God knows what city in Russia or whatever else it is they pretend. Perhaps they are looking for strange things in our afternoon sky, where there are only a few pale gray-and-blue clouds (clouds such as there used to be over the Channel at teatime, when the Boulogne boat pulled into Folkestone harbor).

*   *   *

Brother A., with his frightened-calf look, ready to leave, ready to tear off into any field, has decided to try to make it in the lay brothers and so took the brown habit today. He is more pleased, a little more relaxed, wandering about hoping for approval. I hope he makes it.*

Simone de Beauvoir in her ethic of ambiguity, a harsh ethic where faults are never expiable, sums up Christian ethics thus: "The divine law is imposed upon the believer from the moment he decides to save his soul."

This is exactly the opposite of the New Testament. There is no law for the just man.

Let us see whether Paul is not as good an existentialist as she is! Do we "decide to save" anything? If we do, we soon find out how much we are capable of saving! To save one's soul as object is in fact to cease to have it as an object to save. ("He that would save his soul must lose it.") One must see that "a soul" is not a "thing" one "has"—or "saves." One "saves his soul" by discovering that the soul is what one *is*. Nothing else! To see the soul as "object" or "other" is nothing, zero.

*   *   *

I find considerable moral beauty in the idea, if I have grasped it rightly, that man who seeks vainly to *be* in the fullest sense and accepts to exist in his existence becomes a *revelation of being* for others. This is a very pure notion. It is the function of liberty to make this acceptance of existence rather than being. There is a

*He didn't. T.M.

very Christian temper in existential attitude. We might say in sacrificing his desire to be absolute, man reveals the world to itself as the place of man's meeting with the glory of God in freedom. (The glory of God, the Shekinah, not as an object but as the ground of all presense.)

February 10

Thick wet snow with occasional thunder of jet planes above the snow clouds. Forty hours. Some faculty and students from the College of the Bible were here last evening. Then I was up with the novices for night adoration—quiet, peaceful. An untimely mosquito whined from person to person in the dark, well-warmed church.

*   *   *

Simone de Beauvoir has this to say which corrects so many of the clichés of existentialism: "It is not true that the recognition of the freedom of others limits my own freedom. To be free is not to have the power to do anything you like. It is to be able to surpass the given toward an open future. The existence of others as a freedom defines my own situation and is even the condition of my own freedom" (*The Ethics of Ambiguity*, p. 91).

The question of the open future in Luther's telling critique of religious vows. He is right if the vows are not lived fully and freely! Simply to enclose oneself in "the given" is no glory to God. It is an evasion of life and of growth, a hiding your light under a bushel.

February 11

Crisp snow, cold happy stars. I was reading an ad about caffè espresso with rum in it and was lured by delight! Tomorrow is Ash Wednesday. Thought of caffè poncino—*delectatio morosa*—is a Mardi Gras indulgence, deliberate too!

*   *   *

The warmth and beauty of Anselm's early letters is most helpful and salutary to me. How much I need such exempla, yet how impossible to be quite like that anymore. Our charity must have a different style, just as warm but with less amplitude, I suppose. A simpler expression. His warmth can come to us as sheer gush.

My own letters—the result of harassed efforts to respond to all kinds of strangers everywhere! Of course, there are too many to write to or even to get someone else to write. To some—to friends, publishers, and magazine people—I *must* write, but it is hard to make sense in every letter and typing is difficult because of my numb left hand and sleepy arm. Bad back!

*   *   *

Today, brilliant snow, never so blinding. Pale bright blue sky such as I have sometimes seen in England on rare days in East Anglia. All the trees are heavy with snow and the hills hang like white clouds in the sky. But much of the snow has melted off the trees and there is a slight mist over the sunny valley. No jets, for a wonder, only a train off toward Lebanon. Quiet afternoon. Peace. May this Lent be blest with emptiness, peace and faith!

The woods echo with distant crows. A hen sings out happily at Andy Boone's and snow falling from the trees makes the woods sound as though they were full of people blundering through the bushes.

February 13

One of my great discoveries of this year has been Abbot Ammonas. A magnificent primitive spirituality, the best of the ancient Egyptians with Anthony, whom he succeeded as Abbot of Pispir. We have him in a fascicule in the *Patrologia Orientalis* printed in 1913. No one has ever done anything with it. Ammonas is not even in the dictionaries except DHGE. Hausherr refers to him frequently, however. He should be translated and I should write an article on him.

St. Anselm writes to a monk to meditate on death. He then goes on: "Let no weariness prompt you to give up what you have begun, but go on in the hope of heaven's help and in love of the blessed reward, to undertake what is good for you, that you have not yet attempted, and may you come, led by Christ, to the fellowship of the blessed saints" (Epistle 35).

*   *   *

Fasting clears the head and lessens anguish. Also brings order into one's life.

I think I will try to work on Chuang Tzu finally, but all my resolutions about work go out the window. I never seem to do what I plan. Yesterday, though, I finally finished going over the material to be typed for *Seasons of Celebration*. I don't know whether it is good or not. Perhaps about on a level with *The New Man*.

February 17

After a rainy weekend, warmer days. First week of Lent. Yesterday there was a meadowlark in St. Edmund's field. (Broad sweep of grass and alfalfa with a few oaks against the cloudy sky on the distant hillside.) Today song sparrows around the beehives.

Another Daniel-Rops book in the refectory. It mentioned the medicinal qualities of honey and its part in the diet of the Promised Land. (Naturally!)

February 18

Sometimes a call to spiritual solitude and liberty may come to us masked as a humiliating sickness or weakness. One's weakness or incapacity can itself become that liberty insofar as it humiliates completely. But we do not have the courage to see or admit it, thus we deprive ourselves of that joy. How good God has really been to us and yet we are ungrateful.

February 22

Is Lortz too severe on Erasmus? I was reading Lortz after dinner today and I wondered about this. He keeps saying that Erasmus was "hardly a Christian" and so forth. So Erasmus was a scholar, an individualist! He had not enough sense of the Church, perhaps.

Yet the piety of Erasmus is so clean, so simple and so real. It is a breath of fresh air after so much of the late Middle Ages. In a way, I like it even better than Thomas More's moralism. Was this not what was needed at that time? Is it not completely evangelical?

Erasmus is perhaps one-sided, perhaps lacking in a full Catholic spirit, and maybe he was a danger in many ways. But how can one read him today without joy and agreement? He is a splendid writer and to my mind a deeply pious one. And his satires: are they after all too bitter or too extreme?

One feels that his Catholic critics almost begrudge his fidelity to the Church; as if to satisfy them, Erasmus ought to have apostatized and given them an open-and-shut case against him!

Always the same old narrowness: the Church is regarded as "pure" in the sense of "exclusive"—always excluding what is good but *not quite good enough*! Unfortunately, Erasmus *is* "good enough" still, even by their standards. And they bemoan it!

February 25

I read a hitherto unpublished Greek monastic dialogue in the RAM for 1956. It has some fine things in it. As regards prayer, the last question, number 31 says that when we have done an injustice to another, his grievance stands between our prayer and God and prevents it from reaching God.

This might apply to the world today and the Church in the rich countries. Our fellow man calls out to God against the injustice our system is doing to him. We prosper at his expense. Our concern for him is well meant but illusory. It cannot be efficacious. It can only be a gesture. Yet the Communist power system is in many respects worse. This too is cried out against. Our prayer is not valid unless we are willing to work to change the system we now have, as *Mater et Magistra* and *Pacem in Terris* have so plainly said.

March 3

I had been hoping to republish the few articles on nuclear war, which had been permitted by Dom Gabriel, thinking that it was enough that he had permitted them once. Not so. The new General, Dom Ignace, dug into the files—prompted of course by his secretary, Father Clement, who was Dom Gabriel's secretary—held a meeting of definitors, and declared that there was to be no republication of these articles. Thus, I am still not permitted to say what Pope John said in *Pacem in Terris*. Reason: "That is not the job of a monk, it is for the Bishops." Certainly it has a basis in monastic tradition, which said the job of the monk is to weep, and not to teach. Well, with things here like our cheese business and all the other plangent or weeping functions we have undertaken, it seems strange that the monk should be forbidden to stand up to speak the truth, particularly when the truth in this case is disastrously neglected. A grim insight into the stupor of the Church in spite of all that has been attempted, all efforts to wake her up. It all falls into place. Pius XII and the Jews, the Church in South America, the treatment of Negroes in the U.S., the Catholics on the French right in the Algerian affair, German Catholics under Hitler. All this fits into one big picture, and our contemplative recollection is not very impressive when it is seen only as another little piece fitted into the puzzle. The whole thing is too sad and too serious for bitterness. I have the impression that my education is beginning and only just beginning, and that I have a lot more terrible things to learn before I can know the real meaning of hope. There is no consolation. Only futility in the idea that one might be a kind of martyr for a cause. I am not a martyr for anything, I'm afraid. I wanted to act like a reasonable, civilized, responsible Christian of my time. I am not allowed to do this. I am told I have "renounced this." Fine! In favor of what? In favor of a silence which is deeply and completely in complicity with all the forces which carry out oppression, injustice, aggression, exploitation, war. In other words, silent complicity is presented as a greater good than honest, conscientious protest. This is supposed to be part of my vowed life and this is supposed to give glory to God. Certainly, I refuse complicity. My silence itself is a protest and those who know me are aware of the fact. I have at least been able to write enough to make that clear. I have been able to write enough to define the meaning of my silence. Apparently, I cannot leave here in order to protest, since the meaning of any protest depends on my staying here, or does it? That is a great question. In any case, I have been definitely silenced on the subject of nuclear war. The

letter from Rome also seemed to indicate that the whole book, *Seeds of Destruction*, was stopped, but this must be a mistake, as *The Black Revolution* is appearing this month in France and, in point of fact, the book was permitted.

In a way, I am content. It is certainly a step toward being less public. There is a certain good in drying up and vanishing into the sand but not into their kind of sand, however. I know that this is not even an adventure and it in no way has the mode of happenings that belongs to an adventurer. I have never seriously had adventures or even experiences that happen, that arrive. I don't have the slightest obligation to regard this prohibition as an "event" that has slowly "arrived" here from Rome and reached the point of happening—as it were a puff of smoke signaling the explosion of a non-lethal missile in my immediate neighborhood.

*　　*　　*

One of the things that sickened me the other day when I had a visitor was his implication that we were "having a wonderful time," that some kind of event was taking place which gave life a meaning. What actually happened was meaninglessness in the guise of an event. One must choose, says Sartre, to live or to narrate.

March 4

To narrate: *"raconter."* But this is not a story. It is not an event and I am certain that I need to write in order to stay relatively honest, or perhaps to *become* relatively honest.

Not all writing is narration and one must know when to stop. Certainly one thing is true, much of my writing is useless and the Abbot General's mind, which is not altogether crazy, is rightly aimed against a kind of agitation, an intellectual activism in the order.

I know that to some people I give a distressing impression of agitation and rambunctiousness. That is more their problem than mine, I believe. But I have to be careful to look for the greater good that goes with all obedience and is hidden in it and to see that this care truly does give honor and glory to God. Otherwise, we doubt His wisdom and His power. At the same time, I must

also have a care for the other aspects of His will. That justice be done and truth be defended, leaving to Him the manner in which I am to attempt these things. Hence the thing now is to cut out unnecessary and hasty projects for magazines. Looking back over the peace articles, the truth is that they were ephemeral. There is no need for them to be published in book form now anyway, and a monk should not be writing mere editorials. Again, less writing for quick publication, less writing in debate over immediate controversial issues. More creative writing, deepening of thought, etc.

*   *   *

South wind, thunder and lightning. (There was a cat running in the windy dark through the light cast by the novitiate windows.)

Last night when I came into my novitiate office before going up to bed, there was a copy of a new experimental liturgy in English dreamed up by one of the brothers. It was submitted for me to examine and approve and put over with the abbot. Liturgy and politics! I am not too eager to get involved in either.

*   *   *

Proceeding in peace in the line of God's will, perhaps a deeper Biblical base for such social views as I may have is found in a Protestant writer, A. N. Wilder, who says: "The attitude of the Christian to the world and its institutions will be based on the word of the Cross, upon the good news of God, upon the revelation of the righteousness of God, upon the post-resurrection faith of the disciples . . . not a social ethics based primarily upon the sermon on the mount or on the natural law or on the inner life of the Holy Spirit. Rather the grace of God discloses itself to us in the gospel message and impels us to what we should do to further the purposes of redemption in a world around us" (*The Background of the New Testament in Its Eschatology*, p. 517).

On the other hand, Ida Görres writes in a letter that under pretext of openness to the world, monastic and religious spirit is simply being extinguished in Germany and that last year a Dominican was crowned King of the Fools at Mainz in a carnival on TV. She says her friends in convents who take the ascetic life seriously are the "last of the Mohawks" (sic).

March 6

I received a visit of a Czech Protestant theologian, Jan Milic Lochman. Due to a sudden change of plan, he providentially came to Louisville instead of Richmond, and arranged to come to see me. I had a good conversation, sitting up late with him last night.

We spoke much of Karl Barth and of the fact that Barth is impressed, of all things, with Catholic Josephology! Lochman said that Barth's book on Anselm is one of Barth's own favorites. Barth, like most Protestants, was profoundly impressed by Pope John and said of him that he must make Protestants take another look at the papacy.

Lochman is, of course, an admirer of Bonhoeffer. He twice quoted Bonhoeffer as saying that to qualify to sing Gregorian chant under Hitler, one had to identify himself with the Jews. But Lochman does not go along with a one-sided enthusiasm for Bonhoeffer's plunge into the world that forgets Bonhoeffer's "concentration." Theology in Czechoslovakia and East Germany seems very alive because it has to be a complete expression of life lived in confrontation with and in dialogue with Godlessness. But this confrontation must take place without the privilege of any battlements behind one and without the benefit of a drawbridge. In fact, without any crusade. This is the most important discovery of the Church in those countries. I say the Church, though Catholicism is being slow to discover it. There are still plenty of battlements in Catholic Poland!

It was a very moving and Christian conversation in which we agreed on Christ's word in the world, manifested in the problems that face us, found in the problems themselves, not by evasions from the problems. He spoke of the marvelous way in which a monk of Chevetogne had come to his place and prayed; of the discussions of Catholic and Protestant laymen there; of the great openness that is beginning, and of "In the confusion of man is the providence of God." (I think that is a quote from Luther!) At one moment I felt as if we were sitting together with the hidden Lord in Emmaus, and when I left he gave me an offprint on Bonhoeffer signed "In the joy and fellowship of pilgrims."

March 7

The concept of realized eschatology is very important. It means the transformation of life and of human relations by Christ *now* (rather than an eschatology focused on future cosmic and religious events—the Jewish poetic figures which emphasize the transcendence of the Son of Man).

Realized eschatology is at the heart of a genuine Christian (incarnational) humanism. Hence, its tremendous importance for the Christian peace effort, for example. The presence of the Holy Spirit, the call to repentance, the call to see Christ in man, the presence of the redeeming power of the Cross in the sacraments. These belong to the "last age," in which we now are. But all these do not reveal their significance without a Christian peacemaking mission, without the preaching of the gospel of unity, non-violence and mercy: the reconciliation of man with man and therefore with God. This duty does not mean, however, that there will not at the same time be great revolutionary upheaval.

The preaching of peace by a tiny remnant in an age of war and violence is one of the eschatological signs of the true life of the Church. By the activity of the Church as peacemaker, the work of God will be mysteriously accomplished in the world. The lack of a sense of eschatology is what makes so many Christians fail to see the importance of this Christian duty in the world. Eschatology, having been conceived as purely apocalyptic, having to do only with the end of the historical world, has antagonized Christians. They have turned their back on it in incomprehension and fear, not aware of the true thrust of eschatology, which is here and now.

March 10

Heavy and steady rain with high winds for two days on end, and much rain before that. The Ohio Valley is probably flooded. Here, there is water everywhere. Streams come from everywhere and all night the air is full of the rushing of water and of wind. Wonderful black skies hang over the woods and there is a great strong expectancy of spring in all the wet black trees. There is a yellow waterfall rushing over the new dam down at the waterworks.

*   *   *

Last night I dreamed that a distinguished lady Latinist came to give a talk to the novices on St. Bernard. Instead of a lecture, she sang in Latin with meters, flexes and puncta. Something that sounded like the sermon of the saint, though I could not quite recognize it. The novices were restive and giggled. This made me sad. In the middle of the performance the late abbot, Dom Frederic, solemnly entered. We all stood. The singing was interrupted. I explained in an undertone that I had just now realized that the presence of this woman constituted a violation of cloister and I would remedy matters as soon as possible. Where did she come from, he asked. "Harvard," I said in a stage whisper which she must have heard. Then the novices were all on a big semi, loaded on the elevator, I don't know how, to go down from the top of the building. Instead of the Latinist coming on the elevator, I left the novices and escorted her down safely by the stairs: but now her clothes were all soiled and torn. She was confused and sad. She had no Latin and nothing much of anything to say.

I wonder what this dream is about. Is it about the Church? Is it about the liturgical revival, Anglicanism perhaps? Is it about some secret Anglican anima of my own?

*   *   *

I had a good talk with Dom Aelred Graham, who was here on Sunday. He is very open and sympathetic and one of the most pleasant and understanding people I have run into. A lot of water has gone under the bridge since the *Atlantic* article years ago, in which he severely criticized me and in which no doubt he was not too far wrong. I am grateful that we are now friends. This is a real manifestation of the life of the Church.

*   *   *

Miguel Grinberg, a poet from Argentina, has been here also. Due to the heavy rains, we cannot go out much, so we mostly sit in a room of the guesthouse exchanging ideas and addresses of people we ought to know. He told me about men like Julio Cortázar and other Latin American writers as well as about all the new poetry magazines in South America. The young Latin American poets show wonderful initiative and courage. They are not afraid to publish books on their own and distribute them more or less free. Publishing is cheap. People read poetry: and I mean *people*, not mandarins. I think that this new solidarity, *nueva solidaridad*, is one of the most hopeful signs of life in this hemisphere.

33

* * *

Last night as I was finishing my turn on the night watch, the fire alarm went off and the signal indicated the calf barn, but there was nothing there except bewildered calves and a lot of hay. Everyone turned out in the rain. The brother in charge of the calf barn got there extraordinarily fast and the fire engine dutifully traveled a couple of hundred feet to be right on the scene. There was nothing but rain.

There are floods in Louisville and Cincinnati. Dan Walsh says in Louisville the water is up to Market Street.

* * *

I finished the letters of Anselm this morning and will send back the volumes of Schmitt to West Baden.

* * *

Miguel Grinberg left after we had walked a little on the cold dark hillside to the south of the Farrowing house, taking pictures and talking about more Latin American poets (e.g., Huidobro).

March 14

The other day I saw the floods in Shepherdsville. A drab little town, almost a non-town. Small houses and dark trees standing in the water of the Salt River. The turnpike was not covered and all the cars and trucks of the town were parked on embankments and overpasses where the water could not reach. Total absence of people. They seem to have vanished. They were nowhere except in the newspapers.

March 15, Passion Sunday

It is still cloudy and raining. Two dogs yesterday were worrying a dead woodchuck in the field and disturbed me when I was writing a review of a book on Protestant monasticism. I finally went out and drove them off with stones.

* * *

The calendar in the infirmary refectory shows us now the temple of the emerald Buddha in Bangkok, a "top tourist attraction." Buddha, too, is in the tourist business in spite of himself, along with St. Peter and the Christ of Corcovado, Niagara Falls and Islands in the Sun, old Vienna, Mont Blanc and everything else under the sun.

To insist on living by the Law is to annul and reject the gift of God in Christ (Galatians 3:15–21). It is a refusal to live in and by Christ. More than that, it is a refusal to be Christ in nakedness and simplicity before the Father.

Death is in "living" by the Law, which constitutes me as separate, isolates me in my own judgment and justification, and confirms my isolation by giving me a "standard" with which to judge and reject others.

March 19

I am glad I learned to read at least a little German in school and regret that I have let it go for so long. It is a rich language, the perfect language for an existential theology.

Language has a great deal to do with expressing particular facets of reality. Things can be *discovered* in German that can only be reproduced afterwards in other languages. I am deeply moved, for instance, by the splendid article of Schlier on *Eleutheria* (freedom) in Kittel. It is a superb investigation of the relation of sin, death and works. It explains, for one thing, my own disillusionment and exasperation with the proofs of my new book (*The Black Revolution* again). I am wrong to expect any definitive meaning for my life to emerge from anything that I have done. All it points to is the end: death. Perhaps also, it leads others to deception and hurries them along to their own death. Yet even in this I must witness to life. There are important implications for monasticism in this fine article on freedom. Literal renderings may sound bizarre, but they reveal something.

A few fragments: ". . . Self and others consumed in the Death Might of the own-mighty-life." "The forfeited Dasein—forfeited to self and death—driving from Law to own-life and therefore to death." "Law awakens works which establish one in own-life and therefore make one a gift to death. One draws death to himself in the works that establish one in own-life."

This shows the ambivalence of monastic obedience considered as a justifying "work," which makes me "something" and thereby makes me a prey of death in making me a prey of ambition. But obedience is customarily presented in the monastery as a holy "work" that is pure, that justifies, that is totally disinfected of self. Is this true? What obedience are we talking about? Obedience to a *collective will to power*? To collective self-assertion? To collective might? To collective complacency, ambition, self-satisfaction, self-justification? He who aspires to justify himself by a secret and surefire method is locked in despair and does not know it!

March 21

Today, after several days of laborious work, I finished Schlier's article on *Eleutheria* in Kittel. I am surprised to see how much Zen there is in his insights, which are, nevertheless, so far beyond anything Buddhist, passive or negative. (But is Buddhism passive —negative?) He speaks of the fullest and most positive concept of freedom from death in our death-forfeited Dasein "in which the flesh slavishly wills to attain lordship over itself." Emphasis on the works of love and freedom, on self-forgetfulness that shows us to be free from death because free from concern with self-assertion and self perpetuation, therefore entirely open to others. Close to the root concept of "ignorance" and the "wheel of birth and death" in Buddhism.

March 24

The frightful novel of Piotr Rawicz, *Blood from the Sky*, is a true descent into hell. So much so that it seems to be a voice of Christ, that is, of the not-damned, of the innocent, rising unaccountably out of hell. The innocence of the book in all its horror comes from its realization that *all is sin and horror once you have no mercy*. The relentless, scathing, objective, existentialist revelation of betrayal of the Jews, leaders of their people, by all the wise, all the just, all the capable, all the intelligent and all the holy. A picture of total degradation of everyone and everything—and all of it totally fruitless!

He concludes by stripping off all desire for survival and all love of life, showing it as horror, nausea, hatred, death-dealing selfishness headed inexorably toward its own extinction. A terrible and honest revelation that pulverizes the silly optimism of those Christians who do not take these realities into account. Imagine anyone of our contemporary secular-city optimists addressing himself to those people in the Ukraine and in that situation (under the Nazis). What kind of language could they possibly use?

March 26, Holy Thursday

"All the moral wretchedness, as we see it about us, is *our* wretchedness and *our* weakness" (from Hromadka, in a powerful article about the Christian's concern for the Godless man of today). From such a one I am willing to learn. He says that the obligation of a Christian in socialist society is first to understand that society, to love it and serve its spiritual needs and bring up children in truthfulness and reliability for the sake of helping in the task of building a new world. "Not with groaning but with joyful love for the man of this modern world of ours. We want to bring a service which no one can bring in our stead."

March 27, Good Friday

I came up to the hermitage at 4 a.m. The moon poured down silence over the woods and the frosty grass sparkled faintly in the dark. I had more than two hours of prayer by firelight. The sun appeared and rose at 6:45. Sweet pungent smell of hickory smoke and silence, silence. But birds. Again presence, awareness. Sorry, idiot life. Idiot existence. Idiot not because it has to be but because it is not what it could be with a little more courage and prayer. In the end, it all comes down to renunciation. The "infinite binding" without which one cannot begin to talk of freedom. But it must be *renunciation*, not mere resignation, abdication or giving up. There is no simple answer, least of all in the monastic community. The ordinary answers tend to be confusing. They hide the truth for which one must struggle in loneliness. But why in desperation? This is not necessary.

March 28, Holy Saturday

Nimis amara (exceedingly bitter). These two words jumped out at me from the improperia on Good Friday afternoon. We have all been a most bitter inheritance to our God! (The shameful injustices of South America, especially northeastern Brazil).

More and more I see how we in the Church tend to be deluded and complacent about ourselves. How much there is in our liturgy that puts all the blame on the Jews so that we ourselves enter ourselves, enter into the universal guilt without realizing it. But the improperia are clearly addressed to us. Yet St. Paul says this of the Jews: "What if some were unfaithful, does their faithlessness nullify the faithfulness of God? By no means. *Let God be true, though every man be false*" (Romans 3:3–4). A shattering expression, one of the keys to the New Testament. This is the only genuine basis for ecumenism.

My bitterness is the savor of my own falsity, but my falsity cannot change the fidelity of God to me and to His Church. Hence, I must forget my bitterness and love His fidelity in compassion and concern for all who are without knowing its gall and bitterness in His world. That His joy may change us all and awaken us to His truth and that we may live His truth in fidelity and eliminate injustice and violence from this earth. If we *seek* this, at any rate, He will live in us: but the results are not in our hands.

April 4, Saturday in Easter Week

The Hammers were coming over today but were not able to. It was just as well, for it is cold, dark, windy and threatening.

*   *   *

Last Tuesday workmen began on the new sun porch for the infirmary, which is also at the end of the novitiate wing. There is a lot of noise around here. Hats, pipes, sweaters standing around in a clutter of unassembled concrete forms. The foundation is poured.

I have been reading Paustovsky's *Story of My Life* with pleasure. It is a great book with wonderful warmth and reality.

Kafka is now read in Russia, I hear, and the official people don't know what to make of him now that they understand it is bad form to call him decadent.

Russia is formally and aggressively accused by China of selling out the Communist revolution, which must, when all the chips are down, be a violent one. So the Russians drift back home toward the West. Paustovsky is thoroughly European. He loves Latin and you would be hard put to it to find anyone in America so willing as he to admit this. Yet he is very Russian too.

April 10

Sun, warmth, quiet. A very distant diesel train on the other side of New Haven. Wind in the pine branches. The dogwood buds fatten and grin a little (purple edges of their tiny smile), preparing to open.

*   *   *

The regular visitation of the monastery closed today. Some of my eccentricities were reported to the visitor but I am officially established now in my present offbeat schedule. For instance, because of my back trouble, instead of going to vigils in choir, I remain in bed and take some traction to get the kinks out of my neck and then at about 2:45 a.m. I go to the novitiate chapel for an hour of meditation followed by Lauds. As long as my back is bad, this would seem to be the best thing to do.

Dom Columban, the visitor, wrote a good report, fairly well clarifying the situation of the brothers in transit to the "unified status." Perhaps this will bring a little peace to the community. Meanwhile, I am glad that this official approval, unsought, steers me a little more in the direction of solitude.

April 13

This would be the fiftieth birthday of the worker-priest Father Henri Perrin, if he were still alive. The publishers have just sent me proofs of his autobiography. Actually, it is only a collection of fragments from letters. The fact is, he was driven to despair by the stolid conservatism of the Catholic Church and by its refusal to become detached from sterile commitment to a society that is finished.

As a matter of fact, the whole question is perhaps less complicated than it may seem. So much of the class consciousness, whether left-wing or right-wing in France, is just bourgeois anyhow.

The guilt at "not being a worker" is a purely bourgeois (liberal) guilt.

Henri Perrin is very impressed by the solidarity of the French workers as a class. And everywhere the underlying idea of his book is his need for real solidarity, such as that which he believes can be found among workers, as opposed to the fictitious solidarity of bourgeois individualist Catholics. One gets the impression that he is less concerned with saving the worker by bringing him to the Church than saving the Church by bringing her to the worker. But isn't this because he has to a great extent accepted some myth about "the Worker"?

On the other hand, there is no question that the Church cannot continue much longer in a mere hothouse of comfortable and inane prosperity. One finds very much the same torment of consciousness in Sartre's preface to *Aden Arabie*. A long, garrulous self-examination and confession based on the fact that this book, *Aden Arabie*, by the Marxist Paul Nizan, is itself another version of the same kind of confession.

I have read of a French Jesuit who was brainwashed in China and who gave in to the Communists. I have no trouble imagining what he confessed or did not confess: that he too was a bourgeois and not a worker.

Meanwhile, out of Detroit come some curious documents from Negro Marxist workers with a whole new slant. That, with automation, work is going to become an anachronism and then the worker will have the joy of bourgeois confession too. All this does not alter the fact that Perrin was a brave and serious man, honest and frank about the difficulties of life and honest about the failings of the Church. In general, I think he was quite right.

April 17

This is the second week after Easter. Bright warm days. The Gospel of the Good Shepherd. I have done a lot of work. On Tuesday afternoon I wrote seventeen pages about Gandhi for the little New Directions book. Then I had a kind of hemorrhage in my throat which did not matter or mean anything and it was a beautiful day. I finished the Gandhi piece on Wednesday afternoon, and went over it, making corrections and additions Thursday (yesterday).

*   *   *

Today Marie Tadié called from Paris on the phone. It was the first time I had ever made a transatlantic phone call and one could hear better than in some of the calls from one office to another inside the monastery. *The Black Revolution* is out in France and is apparently doing well, as people in Italy and Spain already want it.

*   *   *

There was a building committee meeting in which the front of the south wing was saved from the indignities that had been planned for it. The new abbatial suite is nearly finished but the machines in the kitchen underneath are creating a problem of noise.

*   *   *

I am reading Rozanov, of whom a new selection has appeared in France. He is an important and dire Christian voice. Shocking and deeply convincing, completely opposed to all the current fashionable optimisms and humanisms. One cannot help listening seriously to his warnings, which are without reservation. True, when he condemns the cosmic joy of Dostoevsky's Zosima, one need not entirely agree; and yet there is some point in what he says. Curious how convincing he is. How he compels assent, at least my assent, even though what he says is so outrageous and so completely contrary to the program of those Christians who have decided to convince the world that we are nice, progressive, alert people.

For instance, he ridicules the cultured monks who claim that they would go to the theater if only the plays were "a little better." (Translate for American Trappists: "We would watch TV if only it were a little better.") There is real originality in Rozanov and a deep religious spirit, even though one cannot accept all his perspectives or all the consequences of what he says. After all, do there have to be Inquisitions?

He has a magnificent piece of writing about Cardinal Rampolla celebrating the Offices of Good Friday in St. Peter's.

Above all, this: "With the birth of Christ and the spread of the Gospel, all the fruits of the earth have become bitter . . . It is impossible not to notice that one can become enthusiastic for art, for family, for politics or science only on condition that one does not look at Christ with full attention. Gogol looked *attentively* at Christ and threw away his pen and died."

This is an extreme yet heartrending statement, and with what art it is made. Of course, everything depends on what you mean by politics. Tsarist careerism perhaps, or a new kind of Byzantine —or Washingtonian—officialism.

Yet the great religious issues today turn out to be also political. Can one look attentively at Christ and not also see Auschwitz?

He would admit that, with his shocking and altogether wrong statement that Christ is the prince of coffins! Yet his sense of the need to turn from the world to God is basically and perfectly right. And he is deliberately paradoxical and ambiguous. After all, one cannot condemn the family or set up the family in opposition to Christ. This is not Christian.

In the end, one does not really see clearly just where Rozanov himself draws the line. His statements are made tentatively, as if he wanted to see what they looked like on paper, as if to state them and let them have a chance to exist in all their outrageousness before deciding whether he really believed them himself. Perhaps I am reading him as if I myself had said these things. Only on such conditions could I myself say them!

April 21

Considerable attention, perhaps too much attention, is being given to the project of six Cistercian monks of Achel (Belgium) who are planning to form a new kind of group and live as contemplatives in the world, as wage earners, on the ground that the well-established business life of the big monastery is contrary to the monastic ideal and creates too much pressure. What I regret most is that this has been made public before they have even been approved. Perhaps approval has been refused them, I do not know. I suppose the last thing they want is publicity anyway. It may be in itself a good idea. There is one ambiguity about it when it is looked at in our American context. That now with automation, the jobs are getting fewer. Should a contemplative monk be taking a job that someone else needs in order to support a family? Again, another big question is: Should a monk be a wage earner? Is this the only honest way to be poor in the present time? I do not know. In any event, there has been a lot of discussion and the new Abbot General, Dom Ignace, has certainly been more broad-minded than Dom Gabriel would have been. The thing is out in the open in the order (although it is not out in the open here at Gethsemani). It is more or less freely discussed outside and there has even been a meeting of abbots and bishops about it.

*   *   *

I have been talking to the novices and juniors about "revision of life," which is perhaps not for us as we now are. There may be something there. I think the real crisis is this: the monk's sense of his own *reality*, his own *authenticity*, the hunger of having a clear satisfying idea of *who* he is and *what* he is and where he stands, i.e., what is the monk's place in the world. (In the world, the monk has no place. He is a stranger and wanderer on the earth. He cannot have the comfort of a clear and respectable identity, can he?) That is precisely the trouble—and the joke—of a place like Gethsemani. Perhaps the formula is still the small farm community like Erlach (in Austria).

April 23

Real spring weather. These are the precise days when everything changes. All the trees are just beginning to be in leaf and the first green freshness of a new smell is all over the hills. Irreplaceable purity of these few days chosen by God as His sign.

I live in a mixture of heavenliness and anguish. Sometimes I suddenly see "heavenliness." For instance, in the pure, pure white of the mature dogwood blossoms against the dark evergreens in the cloudy garden. "Heavenliness" too of the song of the unknown bird that is perhaps here for only one or two days, passing through. A lovely deep simple song. Pure, no pathos, no statement, no desire, just pure heavenly sound. I am seized by this heavenliness as if I were a child, a child mind I have never done anything to deserve, and which is my own part in the heavenly spring. This is not of this world nor is it of my own making. It is born partly of physical anguish which is really not deep, though. The anguish goes so quickly. I have a sense that this underlying heavenliness is the real nature of things. Not their nature, but the deeper truth that they are a gift of love and of freedom, and that *this* is their true reality.

April 24

Heavenliness again. For instance, walking up into the woods yesterday afternoon, it was as if my feet acquired a heavenly light-ness from contact with the earth of the path; as though the earth itself were filled with an indescribable spirituality and lightness. As if the true nature of the earth were to be heavenly; or rather, as if all things in truth had a heavenly existence. As if existence itself were heavenliness. One sees the same thing obviously at Mass but here with a new earthly and yet pure heavenliness of bread. The icons, particularly of St. Elias and his great globe of light and the desert gold, the hard red of the mountain: all transformed. Even in old, hard, cold Rozanov there is a heavenly description of a small store in a side street of Moscow where everybody used to buy onions, dried fish and mushrooms on the first Monday of Lent.

Then there are other things, simple, earthly but not heavenly. Such as roosters crowing at Andy Boone's in the middle of the afternoon; large dogwood blossoms in the middle of the wood that are too large, past their prime, like artificial flowers made out of linen; or the sharp splendid reasonable human prose of the mate-rialist Paul Nizan, describing a man of action in Aden. These things are good but not necessarily heavenly.

Still less quality in Bernard Berenson's diary. I have only dipped into it. It is the diary of an old man for whom the world has made a kind of sense and who knows a lot of people. Barely earthy: just *social*.

April 28
A bright delightful day washed clean of all smoke and dust by two days' rain. Brilliant sky, bird song, hills clothed in their green sweaters. (Brightness of the days and hills at Olean at the cottage, and Lax's poem about Nancy Flagg!)

*　　*　　*

There was a tanager singing like a drop of blood in the tall thin pine trees against the dark pine foliage and the blue sky with the light green of the new leaves on the tulip poplar.

Brightness of sunny hills between Marseilles and Cassis that February morning in 1933 when I started out to walk the coast thirty-one years ago.

The thought of traveling is perhaps soon going to be a real temptation for me, because it may happen sometime that permission to travel may be given. It could indeed be given *now*, but Dom James is so afraid to let anyone out that he never gives permission, although other abbots do. Hence, I must decide and have decided against it. Instead of idly wishing, for instance, that I could visit the Cistercian sites in Wales . . .

Here are two serious invitations that I just received and had to refuse. One to Collegeville in 1965 from Father Godfrey Diekmann. Douglas Steere mentioned this in a letter from Rome the other day. He said he had been talking to Father Häring about how important it was for me to come to this ecumenical conference on the interior life. Permission, of course, refused. Two, to Cuernavaca, where I am now invited by Monsignor Illich for a retreat to be given by René Voillaume and a conference on Latin America. How tempting! I know I would really profit very much from this, but I have obviously no hope of getting permission.

*　　*　　*

I seem to be having trouble with another disc lower in my spine. Considerable pain early yesterday morning and most of the day. It tapered off after I spent some time lying down flat on my back.

For a moment, I was afraid I might have to go back to the hospital. One thing is certain, I am sick and *nauseated* with the futility and excess of my activity. It is all my fault for accepting invitations to do and write things, though in many cases the writing turns out to be profitable.

I am glad I got the article I wrote about *The Deputy* back from Lawler (at *Continuum*). He wants to use it, but I have reconsidered it.

One thing is certain. I am surfeited with words and typescript and print. Surfeited to the point of utter nausea. Surfeited above all with letters. This is so bad that it amounts to a sickness, like the obsessive gluttony of the rich woman in Theodoret who was eating thirty chickens a day until some hermit cured her and brought her to the state where she only ate three.

The only hermit that can cure me is myself, so I have to become that hermit in order to qualify as my own physician. But I have also seen that the cure is going to take time, and if by the end of this year it can be well begun, I can count myself fortunate.

One place to begin is perhaps in the area of letters. All I know is that when I respond to another request asking for a blurb, I feel like a drunk and incontinent man falling into bed with another woman in spite of himself, and the awful thing is that I can't stop.

In the middle of the afternoon, they came to find me in the hermitage and said the editor of a Catholic magazine was there to see me in the monastery and that if I want to . . . the prior had not committed me so I said I could not come. At least I had that much grace and that much sanity. I would only have been involved in more nonsense about some article or other: some pseudoserious crusade. Even if the issue itself were serious, how serious would it be when we all got through mouthing our words about it? I am tired of retching up avant-garde opinions to create the illusion that we are all awake and "forging ahead," "getting somewhere."

*   *   *

This morning I wanted to do some work on the booklet I promised to the monks of Snowmass about the monastic life, but fortunately the Royal typewriter broke down. I took it into the monastery at noon and now I am better off.

April 30

The feast of St. Robert was showery. The workmen were pouring the slab for the infirmary porch. My portable typewriter is in the hands of Father Peter to be fixed. I borrowed Brother Clement's Hermes. A beautiful little machine but I could not find any of the keys. I tried to do a little work on the Snowmass pamphlet in order to get it out of the way, and wrote very badly. I have to see the doctor today, so I will miss a day's work, which is why I am too impatient to get clear of the jobs to which I am committed and become free. But that is not the way.

In the evening of the feast, the dogwood still in full bloom stood out against the dark, distant, horizontal clouds of a clearing sky.

May 1

It was a very cool dawn with a half-moon behind the clouds and a great smell of cow dung around the monastery. Later, when the sun rose hot and brave, the smell was tar and Negroes worked on the roof of the garage. Now, in the afternoon, there is some red machine whacking into the hill in the middle of the horse pasture to make an air hole down into Brother Clement's cheese-curing cave, which someday is also supposed to be a fallout shelter. But this is never fully admitted by anyone.

May 8

I finished the Snowmass pamphlet last Saturday.

Sunday was a good day of recollection. I had a long afternoon outside in the fields alone.

On Monday I had to go to the hospital, St. Joseph's Infirmary, for some tests and the best that can be said of it was that I got back quickly on Wednesday. Hospitals bore and irritate me. Not only that I feel I am trapped when I am in one, not only the noise (they had to give me pills, or I could not have slept because of the traffic on Preston Street), but the sense of being in a totally alien country. A country of ceaseless movement in which things are thought to be happening; where, if necessary, ingenious and complicated happenings are arranged and engage the full-time attention of entire teams of people. (For example, the glucose-tolerance test that I had to take this time.) The best thing about it all was the half day of fasting and the bloodletting. I came back lighter by a couple of pounds (175) and found the monastery full of heat and noise. They were pouring the concrete floor of the infirmary sun porch. I have still not ceased to be tired, but quails whistled in the field and everything is green, for there was much rain yesterday (Ascension Day).

*   *   *

James Laughlin is pleased with the Gandhi book which I sent him a week or ten days ago. That introduction was easy writing. I don't know how the Snowmass pamphlet will look. It is being typed now.

May 12

There is a new loud noise over in the direction of the dehydrator. A kind of mechanical snoring which will probably become, in some way, permanent. Perhaps a new kind of alfalfa chopper. It is very insistent. The same problem of machines here remains unchanged. As we get more used to them, noise increases. Small wonder that Brother B. was in last evening talking about becoming a hermit. I wish there were some way of making this normal for those who seemingly have such a vocation to live a completely solitary life here. But I do think it is becoming gradually possible. Certainly a partial solitude is already available, and I myself have it.

*   *   *

Dom James, home from visitations in the South, is constantly talking about the "bad effect" of sending students to our House of Studies in Rome and gloating over the fact that a "case" is being made out of one. An increasing number of abbots are refusing to send students there, which he himself refused to do for years until forced to by superiors. The main tenor of his argument is—distrust and dislike of the exchange of ideas and of the communication that takes place there and of the fact that men return to their monasteries with "too many new ideas." It is true that some come back with a few bad ideas, but merely stopping all communication and keeping everybody in the dark about what is actually going on is certainly no use.

Brother B. said Dom James is like a man at a desk with wind blowing in through an open window, trying to hold down as many papers as possible with both hands.

*   *   *

There was a Scripture conference in Chapter today. One had the impression of the whole group sinking deeper and deeper into boredom and resignation, until finally at the "discussion" the same dutiful ones as always stood up to speak. The whole place was enveloped in dense spiritual and intellectual fog. Is this irremediable? Perhaps, all things considered, it really is. A community of men dedicated to the contemplative life without too much sense of spiritual realities: earnestness cannot compensate for such a lack. Virtues equal putting up with the despondency which results when they try vainly to hide our collective failure.

May 17, Whitsunday

Yesterday on the vigil of this feast of Pentecost, a group of the Hibakusha on the world peace pilgrimage came out here. They are survivors of the atomic bombing of Hiroshima. Some of them marked by the effect of their wounds. The grass was all cut, the hermitage all swept. A lovely bright day. Everything ideal, except that I had attempted to provide ice water by just providing ice and expecting it to be melted by the time they came to want it; but it had not melted. I was glad to have these pilgrims here. They are men and women signed and marked by the cruelty of this age, bearing in their flesh signs generated by the *thoughts* in the mind of other men. They are a significant indication of what Western "civilized" thinking really means. When we speak of freedom, we are also apparently saying that others like these good, charming, sweet, innocent people will be burned and annihilated if and when we think we are menaced. Does this make sense? Is it not an indication that our thinking is absurdly flawed? True, our thinking is logical and makes war seem right and necessary when it is fitted into a certain context starting from certain accepted axioms; but the trouble is with the context and the axioms. The root of the whole trouble is an entire concept of man and reality itself. This thing has not changed since the axioms have not changed. They are the axioms of sophistry; and sophistry, as Plato knew, spells tyranny and moral anarchy.

It is an illuminating experience to read the last pages of the *Gorgias* and to meet the Hibakusha on the same day. I spoke to them briefly with an interpreter. He translated and explained enthusiastically at great length and I think we were in good rapport, but there was not much discussion.

Dr. Matsumoto, affable and kind, wanted to take pictures and leave in a hurry, as he would have to speak in Louisville in the evening, but the others were not in a hurry. Hiromu Morishita, with his burned chin and his immense shyness, gave me a poem he had written. I did not have a chance to ask him about calligraphy. Nobozu Yamada saw the Sengai calendar and was telling me of the "spiritual principles" on which Idumitsu runs his oil company. Yamada is an old-style Buddhist full of ineffable gentleness and tact. Dr. Namakura—I had little chance to talk to him and he was very shy too. The boy and girl interpreters were full of life and charm. Having grown up *since* the war, they gave a totally different impression. They seemed American-educated, at least. They were much closer to us.

I think the one who impressed me most was the most silent of all, Mrs. Tayoshi. She was always thoughtful, said nothing, kept very much apart and yet was very warm and good. All she did was to come up quietly and with a little smile slip a folded paper crane onto the table after I had read them my poem about paper cranes. The paper crane is the symbol of the Japanese peace movement.

After they had all gone, it was Mrs. Tayoshi's paper crane that remained, silent and eloquent, as the most valid statement of the whole afternoon. I forgot also the newspaper reporter Matsui, a very alert and pleasant man.

It was wonderful to meet all these people. Quite a few other monks and brothers came up to meet them too. They had to leave earlier than we all expected.

May 22

Last day of a Paschal time that has gone by too fast. It is now getting quite warm and tomorrow is Trinity Sunday.

I had a busy week, with one novice leaving after a psychotic breakdown. And another, a postulant, leaving because I knew and he knew that he could not make it here. Then I was over at Loretto, busy with much talking.

Archbishop T. R. Roberts, S.J. was here yesterday. He is neither starry-eyed nor fanatical but is a very solid, radical, clear-thinking person. Certainly frank, and in no sense an ecclesiastical politician. He is outside of all that. He really has something great about him. One of the few, perhaps the only bishop in the Church at present who is an outspoken pacifist. He has got the whole English hierarchy up in arms about birth control by suggesting that the Council ought to reconsider the Church's rigid position on this question of "natural law."

May 26

It is the anniversary of my ordination to the priesthood, already fifteen years. Expecting Zalman Schachter and two other rabbis in the morning, but so far (late afternoon) they have not come.

Lately I have had too many visits and there has been too much talking. Also, I am convinced that I am involved in the wrong kind of talking. A kind of untrue and, in a personal sense, unfaithful playing with modes and perspectives which I do not find as important or as relevant as I seem to when I am talking about them.

This gets back again to my deep unresolved suspicion of activism and of activistic optimism, in which there seems to me to be a very notable amount of illusion. Yet no one speaks intelligently against it. I find in it no stability, no certainty, no deep sense of any lasting reality. This may be due to a lack in my own life. Therefore I am not sure of my misgivings. The fact remains that I feel myself caught and hesitant, indeed, profoundly dubious between the two triumphalisms of the Council: that of the conservatives, the static kind which is obviously absurd, and that of the progressives or the dynamic kind, which after all is sometimes in a frenzy over accidentals (nuns' habits) and is also somewhat naïve in its estimates of the possible future.

Behind this, one senses various possibilities for real intelligence and real concern. For instance, Pope Paul's talk at the Brazilian College read in the refectory today.

May 29

Yesterday, Corpus Christi, was a day of cold, pouring, beating rain, crashing down uninterruptedly through the trees. For the first time there were no complex floral designs in the cloister but only a neat carpet of chopped alfalfa. The smell of alfalfa in the cloister and the church is vile. Some of the older monks were furious about the lack of floral decorations, of course. Furious about the end of formal designs and of all the hullabaloo that went with them!

June 2

More business and more visits. Yesterday afternoon, a long meeting of the abbot's council, the first time there has been serious discussion in the council on the problem of noise around here. In the middle of it all, a call came from Bob Giroux in New York. It appears that the problem of publishing *Seeds of Destruction* is being finally resolved. Giroux wrote to the Abbot General and got a settlement. One essay on war may be printed if I will "transform it." What the "transformation" is, I do not yet know.

*   *   *

Bishop John Gran, the Norwegian Cistercian from Caldey, who is now Coadjutor of Oslo, is here. I had supper with him and Father Abbot and Father Eudes last evening. The conversation consisted mostly of anecdotes about Cardinal Cushing and some talk of monastic questions.

*   *   *

The morning mist is clearing. A sweet dialogue of wood thrushes outside the window. Before the mist cleared, one would have thought the window looked out perhaps on the sea, through the gap in the trees. Now the familiar fields and woods appear but not yet the hills on the other side of the valley.

*   *   *

I am reading about Celtic monasticism, the hermits, the lyric poets, the pilgrims, the sea travelers, etc. A whole new world that has waited until now to open up for me.

*   *   *

I suppose that I am going through another small spiritual crisis. It is nothing new, only the usual anguish and struggle. Perhaps a little intensified by the fact that I am now in my fiftieth year. And yet I think this might be a decisive struggle because now fewer evasions are possible.

As I go on year by year, the ways of escape are progressively closed, renounced, or otherwise abandoned. I know now that I am really committed to staying here at Gethsemani and that even the thought of temporary travel is more or less useless. I know that my contacts with other people of like mind by mail or by visit are also relatively meaningless, though they may have some point and may be fruitful in ways that I do not experience or understand.

I think too that my writing solves nothing for me personally and it has created some problems which remain unresolved. I know there is nothing to be solved or settled by any special adjustment within the framework of the community. My position here will always be ambiguous and my job is to accept this with the smallest possible amount of bad faith. Today I have faced the fact that even if I could obtain permission to live permanently in the hermitage (and I do not now think that under Dom James such permission is possible), it could not be the solution it once appeared to be but only "vanity and vexation of spirit."

However, even if this is true, it is also true that the hermitage is there and that I should make the best use of it, not as a place of escape, but as a real place of prayer and self-renunciation.

*   *   *

I am reading the little book of Eberhard Arnold of the Bruderhof, a Protestant Evangelical community, and I think this statement written on his fiftieth birthday applies well enough to me. I can almost take it as a word of God to me. "Let us pledge to Him that all our own power will remain dismantled and will keep on being dismantled among us. Let us pledge that the only thing that will count among us will be the power and authority of God in Jesus Christ through the Holy Spirit, that it will never again be we that count but that God alone will rule and govern in Christ and the Holy Spirit."

June 12

Full summer heat, blazing and stifling. It is not cool anywhere, either at the hermitage or in the monastery; although the novitiate generally gets a cool breeze from the forest to the northwest, even on the hottest days. It has been a busy week. I finished the rewriting that I was required to do for the peace section of *Seeds of Destruction* and also wrote two new poems.

*   *   *

A surprise! After writing as I did the other day that I thought even temporary travel would be useless to think about, I received a letter Wednesday from the secretary of the Japanese Zen scholar D. T. Suzuki. She said that Suzuki was going to be in New York this month and that he could definitely not come to Gethsemani but he really wanted to meet me and could I come there. I thought about this, and since it is probably the only chance I will ever have to speak to him, I thought it was important enough to ask the abbot's permission. I certainly did not think that Dom James would give this permission and yet, very hesitantly, he did and a flight is booked for me next Monday, the 15th of June. Since this decision has been reached, I am distracted and confused, except for the real joy of seeing Suzuki. I can think of nowhere I would less like to go than New York. I will stay on the Columbia campus somewhere, probably at Butler Hall, out of the midtown section where I would meet friends. That is all right!

I have been put under strict obedience not to see anybody but Suzuki, or to let anybody else know that I am in New York.

June 13

Rain in the night at bedtime, rain in the morning at early Mass, the Mass of Our Lady. At the Last Gospel I could see the blue Vineyard Knob in the gray west with a scapular of mist on its shoulder. Then, during Thanksgiving, those other knobs! The pointed one, the woods, of which I never tire. Is it really true that I have no "place"?

The little poplar tree I planted on the west side of the novitiate chapel in 1957 or '58 is now up to the second-floor windows and I saw great drops of rain sitting on the fat leaves after the rain had stopped.

Where will I say Mass in New York? Corpus Christi probably.

Last night I dreamed I had found a cool clean convent of nuns on West 114th Street near where I used to have my rooms.

I seem to think less about Suzuki than about a million trifles. Will I get to the Guggenheim Museum? Will I find all the Klees in the Guggenheim Museum? Will I find Rajput painting and Zen drawings at the Metropolitan? Or will I perhaps slyly get to a concert?

June 15

I am all shaved and ready to go, after I get the abbot's blessing and some money. I am not sure whether I look forward to the trip with pleasure or with joy. It could be unpleasant. The mere thought of New York gives me stomach spasms. Anyway, New York is in a ferment with racial trouble, and Columbia is right over Harlem, where there has been violence on a small scale recently.

June 20

The first thing about New York was that I was delighted to see it again. I really was. I recognized Sandy Hook immediately from the air and saw the big new bridge over the Narrows. So much recognition everywhere right down to the two big gas tanks in Elmhurst. Landmarks of all my family funerals from Mother's to Aunt Elizabeth's, to Pop and Bonnemaman. (We passed these on the way to the cemetery.)

When the plane took off from Louisville and was climbing up above the clouds, the hostess came and asked my destination. I said "New York," and as soon as I said that, there was a great joy in my heart because, after all, I was going *home*!

I remember sitting in Butler Hall on the thirteenth floor. I was given apartment 13Q for two nights and watched the sunset and sunrise over Harlem.

Meditated, looked out toward Long Island Sound, where it was clear, and watched the red lights go on and off on top of the stacks of a big power plant in Long Island City.

There was shooting in Harlem most of the night and I found out two factions of Black Muslims were fighting. It was not all secure and respectable around Butler Hall. There had been murders and muggings everywhere. The last day I was in New York a man was murdered in an elevator in an apartment house in the Nineties. The taxi driver told me that on the next block to Butler Hall were many junkies and criminal types.

*　　*　　*

I had two good long talks with Suzuki. He is now ninety-four, bent, thin, deaf but lively and very responsive. Much support from Miss Okamura, his secretary, who is very charming and lively. They both were extremely friendly. Apparently Suzuki had read several of my books and it seems quite a few Zen people read *The Ascent to Truth*. That is somewhat consoling, though it is my wordiest and in some ways emptiest book. Or, in any case, it is a book about which I have doubts. I think the material in it may be fairly good, but it is not my kind of book, and in writing it, I was not fully myself.

Suzuki was especially pleased with my essay on Zen in *Continuum* and thought it was one of the best things on Zen that has been written in the West. Miss Okamura made the green tea and whisked it up in the dark brown bowl. I drank it in three and a half sips, as prescribed, and found it wonderful. I was pleasantly surprised. (James Laughlin had said, on the contrary, that it was awful.)

So I sat with Suzuki on the sofa and we talked of all kinds of things to do with Zen and with life. He read to me from a Chinese text, the Blue Cliff collection, I think, familiar stories on Zen. I translated to him selections from Octavio Paz's Spanish version of Fernando Pessõa. There were a few things in Pessõa he liked immensely (especially "Praise be to God that I am not good"—"That is so important," said Suzuki with great feeling).

Suzuki likes Eckhart very much, as I already know from the book of his that I got at the University of Kentucky several years ago.

These conversations were certainly pleasant. It was profoundly important to me to see and experience the fact that there really is a deep understanding between myself and this extraordinary and simple man, whose books I have been reading now for about ten years with great attention. I had a renewed sense of being "situated" in this world. This is a legitimate consolation. He told a story which was new to me about Hakuin's dream of his mother. The mother appeared to him with two mirrors. One in each sleeve. The first one was black and the second contained all things. Hakuin looked again at the first one: in it he saw all things *and himself among them, looking out.*

* * *

I tried to explain things that perhaps did not need explaining and we both agreed on the need to steer clear of movements to avoid promoting Zen or anything else. Miss Okamura seemed very eager about this too and she obviously knows her Zen. For once in a long time I felt as if I had spent a few moments with my own family. The only other persons with whom I have felt so much at home in recent years are Victor Hammer and his wife, Carolyn. It was rather like one of the visits with the Hammers. (I hear Victor is about to have an operation for cataracts.)

* * *

The evening before flying home by an early plane, I moved downtown to a hotel (the Tuscany), close to the East Side Air Terminal. I listened to FM radio, went to Le Moal for supper and had a very good one with a couple of glasses of wine and some Bénédictine. On the way down I stopped in at the Van Gogh exhibit at the Guggenheim Museum. The only thing I found really irrational about the place is that most of the pictures are not hung but in storage. Hence, I could see nothing of Klee or of Miró. Alas!

*   *   *

Coming home, we took off over the Atlantic and got above a thick bank of clouds over Jersey and I read a book, *The Friends of God*, which I had borrowed from a Columbia library. When the clouds cleared, I watched the long thin ridges of the Appalachians in West Virginia. Then we bounced through thunderstorms over eastern Kentucky and came down to Louisville in rain and muggy heat. I went to say Mass at Carmel. For two mornings in New York, I said Mass entirely by myself at Corpus Christi, without a server. Deeply moved to say Mass at the altar of Our Lady, before which I made my profession of faith twenty-six years ago. No one recognized me or discovered who I was. At least I think not.

*   *   *

June 23

It is blazing hot. The air is stuffy, barely moved by a little breeze here in the woodshed. What a day it is going to be. Even the woods will be an airless furnace. It calls for one of those nature poems. A kerygma of heat such as the Celts never had. (I just finished Kenneth Jackson's excellent book, *Early Celtic Nature Poetry*, before Prime, as the fierce sun began to burn the fields.)

*   *   *

My first real interest in the "Honest to God" problem is beginning to show. Is this really something new? I think the problem is real enough and it is even one which Christianity has, in fact, faced since the beginning. But the solution of the Bishop of Woolwich tends to be a collapse, a complete surrender to nonsense and confusion. Is it true that man is now totally and complacently content with modern technological culture just as it is? What, then, is the difference between this kind of acceptance and Eichmann's acquiescence? I don't know. One must not stop at appearances and judge everything by a few "God is dead" texts taken out of context.

58

June 26

Feast of SS. John and Paul. I said a Mass for John Paul, my brother (and included Sartre in it!).

It is cooler. Two great pigeons set up shop in the rafters of the woodshed and, with gurgling and cooing and beating of wings, make the place more delightful. This morning they were playing some kind of serious love game together, flying around the gutters and then looking at me through the cracks between the gutters and the roof.

I finished the book *The Friends of God*, which I am returning to Columbia. I will never forget reading the chapter on the "book of the nine rocks" while flying over the Appalachians. I must try to find out more about this subject.

In the afternoon, I wrote a note on the poems of Kabir for the *Collectanea*.

June 30

Serious problems in the Church. What a shame that all through the Church the "will of God" can so easily resolve itself into the will of an Italian undersecretary in the Holy Office. In fact, the conservative Vatican bureaucrats are serenely convinced that they have the right to override the Pope himself. *They* are the ones who are really infallible!

The mystique of infallibility joined with conservatism and power politics may lead to a colossal crisis of order and obedience throughout the whole Church. When will it really break? I don't know.

There are curious similarities with the conservative pattern in the South of the U.S. The ruthless defiance of law and order by those who are convinced that their own fantasies represent the only true concept of law and order, and who think that their own mystique of society is sacrosanct. Following their own irresponsible whims, they are undermining law and bringing about anarchy.

How badly we need a real spirit of liberty in the Church! It is vitally necessary. The whole Church depends on it. There is an appalling scandal in the way in which the whole idea of the Church's authority is undermined by Church politicians. This even raises (once again) serious questions about my own vocation. Certainly I do not doubt Providence, but just as certainly I cannot really let a strict political pragmatic and juridical answer be the final word and prevent me from doing what I believe God wants me to do, that is to say, live in greater solitude. But, in any case, I do have the hermitage to go to for part of the day. The important thing is the understanding and the resolution of doubts and misgivings.

July 8

I do not at all like President Johnson's policies in Asia. To make sure of votes in this year's Presidential election, he has to threaten war and promise "results" against the Communists. There is something very strange about a system where a political power for a party or an individual demands the sacrifice of lives and of poor people thousands of miles away, people who never even heard of Democrats or Republicans. I am not talking about Communist power only, but power of Democrats and Republicans. Can I honestly vote for anyone in this year's election? All the future promises is the possibility of a long, stupid, costly, disastrous and useless war in Asia. It will certainly bring no good whatever to anyone, but because it does not involve a nuclear threat to the U.S., everybody shrugs and thinks about something else.

July 10

Thinking back on many things that I saw those few days in New York, especially the rainy streets around Columbia on that first evening. Amsterdam Avenue wet, empty, a few cars and buses speeding along and a tall girl with long white bare legs and a little black jacket hurrying to Johnson Hall. Perhaps a German student.

The trees along 116th street, the dark comfort of rainy trees and of their shadow and half shelter. Foreign students everywhere. The comfort of hearing foreign languages, French, German, Polish and Puerto Rican Spanish.

The new Asian restaurant and the gray-haired Chinese waiter who had seen everything. Pork and fried rice; thin tea and egg dip soup. I was hot and wet. I ate gladly but there was too much food! Too much also the next day at lunch at the College Inn. Too much

Japanese food for supper at the Aki next to Butler Hall (bits of eel, bits of chicken, etc., floating in a nice broth, rice in a wooden bowl, green tea). I was hot and wet in the Aki. Many Japanese faces. Earnest Japanese student talking to an American student there by the window. Not much air. Hot and wet in the Paperback Store. Too many books. I was glad to get back to Butler Hall and have a bath and sit in pajamas on the floor looking out over Harlem, listening to all the sounds and the shooting and drinking cheap sherry wine on the rocks. A lovely vacation.

On the Wednesday I was in New York, it was a lovely morning and at noon I rode down in the taxi to the Guggenheim Museum through the park under tunnels of light and foliage, with the driver talking about his problems, his nerves, his analysis and his divorce. The more I think about the museum, the more I recognize it as a light, beautiful, airy and intelligent place. And the Van Goghs, wheels of fire, cosmic, rich, full-bodied honest victories over desperation, permanent victory, especially the last light-and-shadow calligraphic impastos. But the Metropolitan Museum was zero. I was in and out of an old world, an old station that I had passed through long ago. The people walking on Fifth Avenue were beautiful and there were those familiar towers of hotels along the Park. The street was broad and clean, a stately and grownup city, a true city, life-size! A city with substance and scale, large and bright, well lighted by sun and sky. Anything but soul-less. New York is feminine. It is she, the city. I am faithful to her. I have not ceased to love her to the last gasp of this ball-point pen, the gift of the Nazionale Distributing Co., distributors of Stroh's and of Schlitz in Follansbee, West Virginia. (Pen runs out!)

New pen! Down at the end of Park Avenue, shadows, darkness, noise, crowds, traffic and a building being destroyed. In the mornings it was wonderful walking to Corpus Christi (and coming from Corpus Christi), walking in the sun and wind of Broadway along the Barnard fence or behind Earl Hall, where I remember all those medical examinations. The pleasant place for breakfast near the library called Campus Corner, where the waiters were having an angry argument and suddenly ceased, abashed by the presence of a priest.

Then going to work at the library catalogue, finding almost everything I looked for. It was an experience to go to a library and find almost everything you look for. It is not that way in Louisville!

*   *   *

Some conclusions: Literature, contemplative solitude, Latin America, Asia, Zen, Islam, etc., all these things come together in my life. It would be madness for me to attempt to create a monastic life for myself by excluding all these. I would be less a monk. Others may have their way of doing it but I have mine.

July 12

I am deeply moved by Adomnan's extraordinary life of St. Columba. It is a great poetic work in its own way, full of powerful symbols, indescribably rich. Through the Latin (which is deceptive and strange too) appears a completely non-Latin genius. The prophecies and miracles are presented not as signs of *authority* but as signs of *life*. That is to say, they are not signs of power conferred on a designated representative (juridically), a delegated power from outside of nature, but rather a sacramental power of a man of God, who sees and experiences the divine in God's creation. Thus, the miracles of St. Columba are words of life spoken in the midst of life, not words of power breaking into life and silencing it, making it irrelevant by the decree of absolute authority (replacing the authority of life which life receives itself directly from its own Creator!).

July 14

A fruitful evening yesterday when I drove with Father Prior (Flavian) to meet Abraham Heschel at the airport. It was a fine sunny afternoon, cool, with the hills all green and splendid. There was much noise in the airport, a broadcast of the Republican Convention, where Goldwater will obviously be nominated. One of the first things that Heschel said was that he was disturbed at this incredible event. Heschel, of course, went through the Nazi persecution and was very fortunate to escape with his life.

There were at least a half-dozen Loretto nuns around the airport, meeting other Loretto nuns coming for their General Chapter, which opens today. A fine day for it!

Riding back in the car and at supper, we talked over many things. Of his new book, *Who Is Man* (not *what* is man), and of the basic sin, which is idolatry. Two rabbis argued as to what was the greatest commandment, love of brother or prohibition of idolatry. Both are right. I would be inclined to think that the prohibition of idolatry was more fundamental, since when one has "an idol" (and any god that stands in the way of loving one's brother is an idol), one can permit oneself to sacrifice everything to it, including truth, love, justice and one's brother. The function of this idol is to *permit everything*, provided the idol itself receives unconditional adoration. Heschel was talking about a rabbinic commentary on the phrase "other gods," that is to say, "gods that are always changing." Gods that are "always other," gods "made by others" and so forth. To have a god other than the true God is to be alienated; an idol is a principle of alienation. Heschel thinks that the Jewish Chapter will never be accepted by the Vatican Council. We spoke of how symbolic this fact was. In my opinion, the acceptance of this Chapter and the consequent implicit act of repentance is necessary for the Church. In reality, the Church stands to benefit more by it than the Jews. Heschel said, "Yes, but when I was a child I was beaten up often by Catholic Poles for being a Christ killer and I want to see that fewer Jewish children are beaten up for this reason." He thinks that Cardinal Bea is practically finished and that he suffered a crushing defeat in the Second Session. The envy aroused by Bea's American trip brought him many enemies in Rome and he already had many before.

Heschel is very impressed by Monsignor Willebrands, now a bishop. He has much hope in him. He does not attach much importance to the new secretariat for non-Christian religions. I sat up until 10:30 talking with Heschel after a good supper fraught with dietary problems too great for Brother Edwin to solve, but Heschel did well on cheese and lettuce. He enjoyed the wine and smoked a couple of enormously long cigars.

* * *

This morning before High Mass, Brother Patrick, the abbot's secretary, told me that a letter from the definitor, Dom Laurence, had come and the long section on peace for *Seeds of Destruction* had been passed without change by the General. Thus, the real heart of the once forbidden book, "Peace in the Post-Christian Era," is to be published after all. This could never have happened if Dom Gabriel had not been so tough on those other three articles which would have been used in *Seeds of Destruction* if he had not forbidden their reprinting. Thus, in effect, the very thing he wanted to prevent most has happened because of his own authoritarianism and intransigent use of power. This is something to remember when we think of religious obedience. The Church is not entirely run by officials. None of this was arrived at in the end by any rebellion or initiative of my own. Again, the part of the present General, Dom Ignace, demanding that I rewrite the one article which the publisher tried to insist on, led to this whole new approach. How strange are the ways of God.

*   *   *

Brother Alfonse, the Ecuadorian novice, has his arm in a cast with a broken elbow. Brother Eugene, a novice from Texas, drawls, goes about with his hands in his pockets and is for Goldwater because Goldwater "knows where the money comes from and is for the individual." These are our two postulants of this summer. Another younger one is to come later from a farm in Michigan. And it was decided yesterday that a Jesuit from a Detroit province did not have a vocation to our life. Dom James is ruthless in excluding Jesuits from the monastery.

This afternoon, I am to talk to one who was a postulant in the big group in 1957 and who left after an appendicitis operation. Perhaps he wants to reenter. How many of those who entered then are still here. I can only think of ones that have gone.

I do not want to make a crisis of these departures, but they are significant. Others would say they are ominous, but for what? For the big institution perhaps, but not simply for monasticism.

July 18

The story of St. Brendan's voyages. The *Navigatio S. Brendani* came yesterday from Boston College library. I began it this morning, studying it as a tract on monastic life. The myth of pilgrimage, the quest for the impossible island, the earthly paradise, the ultimate ideal. As a myth it is, however, filled with a deep truth of its own.

A Cuban exile who does not speak English is here to be a family brother but I do not think he will be able to settle down. He speaks of Castro with fury.

July 19, Ninth Sunday after Pentecost
The sun is rising in streaks of dirty mist.

If I had never seen a Japanese print, I would probably have experienced this in a purely Western way. The sun as one thing among many, a multitude of trees, enclosure wall in the foreground. But Sumiye makes this whole view *one*. One—a unity seen because the sun is in the center, a unity which is more than the total of a number of parts.

In the infirmary kitchen there are atrocious printed photos from paper companies to advertise the quality of their litho paper. Emphasis on bright color. Colored objects without composition, without sense. Dolls, flowers, toys, food. Food, food, food. Immense hamburgers. Chocolate icing in a bowl, etc. All thrown at your head. Total barbarity!

Last week Goldwater was nominated on the first ballot at the Republican Convention. Made statements and issued a platform which were supposed to sound reasonable.

July 21
It has been cool. Today will probably be hot, as the sun looks red and angry through early haze and one can barely discern the knobs (which a novice referred to, the other day, as "the Appalachians") across the valley. I have written an article on "Honest to God" and sent it to the *Commonweal* yesterday.

*   *   *

Really, Bonhoeffer is far deeper than you would imagine from reading about him in Robinson. I am reading Bonhoeffer's *Prison Letters*, which are very monastic in their own way. I would like to make a collection of some of the monastic statements from these letters. His "worldliness" can only be understood in the light of this "monastic" seriousness, which is, however, not platonically inward. It is not a withdrawal, a denial. It is a mode of presence. Paradoxically, then, Bonhoeffer's mode of unnoticed presence in the world is basically monastic as opposed to the "clerical" or "priestly" presence, which is official, draws attention to itself and issues its formal message of institutional triumph. That is the trouble with the Bishop of Woolwich. He is too concerned with "the message" and in the end he seems to be saying that he has discovered a new sales pitch that will work better than the old ones. If that is so, he is wasting his time, except that a few others like him may derive comfort from his message. His whole problem seems to boil down to that of being needed in the world even when he begins to admit that he may not be needed.

Graham Greene's *Burnt-Out Case* takes this up a bit savagely and very well. The complete burning out of Christianity in the official clerical sense is the subject of the book. Not a great book, but still it is timely, urgent, convincing.

Greene knows what he is saying. Burning out the appetites of a bourgeois world, sexual, cultural and religious. The appetite for life. Pfft! On the back of this paperback is the usual inane comment about that same mythical other book which is the one the salesmen sell and not the one that the author wrote. *"He was famous, she was lonely!"*

*   *   *

I finished my first reading of the Voyage of St. Brendan this morning. Interesting monastic vocabulary. Is the geography of the journey a liturgical mandala? I have to check back on the significance of directions. North is liturgical hell here too and the promised land is West, except that in reference to the paradise of the birds, it is East, which is more liturgical. Perhaps we have a convergence of two traditions.

July 23

Jim Forest sent me clippings from Monday's *New York Times* about the big riots in Harlem last weekend. It all took place in the section immediately below Butler Hall from 116th to 130th Streets between Eighth and Lenox Avenues. I can picture the houses, the roofs, and the streets now, and I can imagine the racket. The police shot thousands of rounds into the air but also quite a few people were hit and one man on a roof was killed. In the middle of all the racket and chaos and violence, a police captain was shouting, "Go home, go home," and a Negro yelled back, "We *are* home, baby."

*   *   *

Greene's *Burnt-Out Case* is not much of a book really. It is competent but it is itself a bit burned out and silly. Yet one reads it with interest. Same problem as in "Honest to God" but turned around. The priest who insists that Querry is not an atheist but is really in the dark night! All of a sudden one realizes that this approach has now become so usual that it is a cliché. Indeed, it is Greene's own mainspring. Most of his novels seem to work on this idea and here it is very tired indeed, yet it still works—more or less.

*   *   *

I am very impressed and deeply moved by Ramana Maharshi. Not only by his life, of which I know only the bare outline, but by his doctrine (traditional Advaita), or rather by his experience. Whatever may be the deficiencies of the doctrinal elaboration and the misleading effect of some of his philosophical concepts, this is the basic experience. God as the ultimate self, who is the Self of every self. It is this that Christianity too expresses in and through the doctrines of grace, redemption, incarnation and the Trinity. We are sons in the Son by grace. We recognize the Father as Him with whom we are one, not by nature but by His gift.

But the impact of Maharshi's experience awakens in us the real depth of this truth and the love that springs from it. How powerless so much Christian writing and teaching is today in this respect. How lost and how far off the real target! The words are there, the doctrine is there, but the realization is absent. Maharshi has an inadequate doctrine perhaps, but the real realization.

July 28

It is very hot and damp. We are getting our real hot weather now. Last night, storm and rain in the middle of the night. I was awakened by a mosquito and then a jet went roaring over low down in the rain, and through the shutters I could see the lights swinging rapidly away eastward. Probably one of the SAC planes, for one has been going over regularly at that time, about 1:20 a.m.

Interesting background on the Voyage of Brendan. Its connection with the monastic reform in Lorraine in the tenth century. There are a few fine paragraphs from the life of Bruno, Archbishop of Cologne, about his love of learning, and of scholars, both Irish and Greek. The *Navigatio* is using Celtic myth as a hook on which to hang a manifesto of spiritual renewal in monastic life, both eremitical and cenobitic.

Children from the Christian Church of Carrollton, Kentucky, were here. Good, simple children, open, unspoiled, not frightfully interesting, but I felt a kind of compassion for the simplicity they will probably lose. I think of their little town on the Ohio. I think what, I don't know. Emptiness. These children are relevant only in emptiness as soon as one begins to specify . . .

August 2, Eleventh Sunday after Pentecost
It is very hot, steamy and clammy. The tropics have nothing we don't have here in summer except thicker vines and more spectacular snakes. We are friends of the king snake around the novitiate and the hermitage. The *Commonweal* intends to print my article on "Honest to God" if the censors don't stop it. There have been riots in Rochester. I finished Bill Stringfellow's book on Harlem and will write to Joe Cuneen about it. It is first-rate. Full, especially, of important information. How the political machinery works to maintain inertia, how the rent system works, and so on. It becomes clearer and clearer what a sick system this is: but anonymous. If there were one sick king, he could be deposed and replaced but here "they" operate and get rich; and it is never quite clear who "they" are or how they get so rich.

*   *   *

I finished my essay on "Pilgrimage and Crusade."

Ulfert Wilke, the abstract artist, was here the other day and we discussed drawings, talked about some of the ways of mounting and framing some of the calligraphies I have been doing. I want to see his new paintings. He spoke of Ad Reinhardt and of some Japanese artists that he knows.

August 3

Hottest day yet. Sweat all over everything. It is difficult to get any work done.

*   *   *

Someone has sent a book, *African Genesis*. I had heard of the discoveries of Leakey at Olduvai and was prepared to accept the hypothesis of Africa as the cradle of the human race. This book, however, takes scientific hypotheses and creates a myth of violence around them and in them. Man's ancestor is said to be the meat-eating, club-carrying, sinister killer ape who fought his way up from vegetarianism in order to become a cannibal and/or a nationalist. These, says the myth, are the true facts. And when the myth says that, it means, of course, the only fact. So man is by essence a predator, a killer, a property owner, a hater, a joiner, an agitator, perhaps even a Goldwaterite. This is the scientific mythology of protofascism. With all that, I am quite willing to accept Leakey, with a different and less romantic story of anthropoids that used tools and weapons and were perhaps already men.

August 5

It is difficult to read or hear the story of Port Royal without having a great deal of sympathy for the Jansenists. Wrong as they may have been, there was a rightness that the heart knew and clung to. This was dangerous, no doubt, but were the others much less so? We are hearing in the refectory about this from Daniel-Rops.

*   *   *

I have been sending out a mimeograph memorandum on monastic reform and evidently Dom James does not like it. He has not said anything to me personally, but his Chapter talk yesterday was all about heresy, intellectual pride and the downfall of "Dr. Martin

Luther, Ph.D.," not to mention Judas Iscariot. His usual approach when someone disagrees with his ideas. If that was prompted by my paper and letter to Dom Leclercq, which was obviously read by the abbot on its way out, then it must be an indication that he is afraid I am right. Does it matter so much? I am not going to get into controversies, and even the whole question of monastic reform seems to me to be full of illusions. The time of real and serious reforms, it seems, is not yet or at least not *here*. Doubtless, something may begin somewhere else. There are places like Erlach. My article "The Monk in the Diaspora" is making more noise and perhaps raising more trouble than I anticipated.

*   *   *

I hear that the bodies of the three young civil-rights workers, murdered in Mississippi in June, have been strangely found in an earth dam which was leaking because the bodies were there. A strange and macabre significance!

Today in Chapter, Father Abbot announced that there was trouble with the Pacific Fleet off Vietnam. Those big bullies of North Vietnam had attacked the Pacific Fleet with a PT boat, which had to be destroyed, and now "the nest" from which the bullies are sending out these boats to attack and persecute our fleet must also be destroyed. In an election year it almost seems inevitable that the politicians and generals will get what they want: the bombing of North Vietnam. Sheer waste, nonsense and criminal stupidity, but what can one do about it? Who listens to protests?

August 9

The other day in Louisville I picked up W. H. Auden's *Enchafèd Flood* at the library. It is good background for the Voyage of Brendan. I must finally reread Melville, but when does one get time for all these things? It all depends, I suppose, how badly I want to read Melville and how guilty I will feel about doing so, but actually there is no need to feel guilt. *Moby Dick* has a great deal to do with the monastic life and perhaps a great deal more than the professedly spiritual books in the monastic library. Perhaps unwisely I have consented to do an article on "Art and Morality" for the *New Catholic Encyclopedia*. One reason why I consented was that the editor of the section is Ned O'Gorman's friend, the Benedictine artist.

*   *   *

Yesterday morning I said Mass in the middle of a thunderstorm and then it got cooler. The afternoon was bright and serene. I got back to a decent meditation which has not been working well in the heat. I find that in an hour's meditation I tend to be sleepy for the first twenty minutes or so. Not asleep but dazed in a kind of total blackout: but then after that everything gets very clear. So yesterday the twenty-minute blackout seemed to be a necessary passage from confusion to truth, a recovery from pressure and movement, a return to balance. Before that, I am not awake. I am just moving around.

*   *   *

I am finishing *The Plague* by Camus in French. It is a precise, well-built, inexorable piece of reflection. A picture of white society as it really is when undefended by distraction. I can accept Camus's ideas of nobility and certainly agree with him about the sermon of the Jesuit. Yet the nobility of the doctor is still not enough, though it may be enough for the doctor and that may be all that most men can do. There is some nobility in the simplification of reasons in the renunciation of religious explanations: but to live without ideology is not to live without faith. This doctor would not be possible without the Gospel or without some cryptic compassion that is more than simply humanistic. Has Camus got far beyond Kant?

*   *   *

Raïssa Maritain, in her book on Chagall, speaks of the light of New York—the best light for seeing Chagall's paintings. I agree. I was struck by that light again this June. So much clearer, braver, more uncompromising than the light of Louisville, which is a vague town.

The Plague of Camus is more understandable in the light of Bonhoeffer's admirable prison letters. Take, for example, this line of Bonhoeffer and compare it with Camus: "I often ask myself why a Christian instinct frequently draws me more to the religionless than to the religious, by which I mean not with any intention of evangelizing them but rather, I might almost say, in brotherhood."

August 12

For St. Clare, after days of heat, a cool gray day with lovely wind blowing through the dark novitiate chapel before dawn, and dark clouds most of the morning. It was almost cool in the garden. Instead of writing letters, I began some conference notes on art for the novices, somewhat against my own better judgment, and yet they seem to be needed. Also I already have materials and ideas for the *New Catholic Encyclopedia* article but no time to write it. Maybe next week.

*   *   *

Last night I dreamed that Dom James suddenly announced that we would have formal "military parades for the dead," along with every Office of the Dead now. Monks would march in spaced ranks slowly through the church *for a long time*. I saw this begin and saw that the sick monks were all forced to participate. Indeed, even the dead were in it, for Father Alfonse was there, though he was stumbling a great deal.

The abbot was absolutely insistent on this preposterous new observance as a firm manifestation of his will. I tried to reason with him and said it was a violation of monastic simplicity. I even tried to find a copy of *The Spirit of Simplicity* for him to read but I could not find one anywhere.

August 24

A wonderful sky all day, beginning with the abstract expressionist Jackson Pollock dawn. Scores of streaks and tiny blue-gray clouds flung like blotches all over it. Before my conference (on liturgy and on a recent Reinhold article), deep clear blue sky with astonishing small luminous clouds, than which I never saw lighter and cleaner! Exhilarating coolness and airiness of these little clouds!

*   *   *

I have to prepare a talk to give at the meeting of the American abbots here in October and I am supposed to think up something to say about the ability or inability of young modern postulants to settle down in our kind of life. It is a real problem. A question of identity. I suppose I will have to talk on identity crisis.

People come here often seeking their own identity, and find themselves in a life that explicitly frustrates the quest of identity. When we only half understand our Rule and apply it rigidly and wrongly, we arrive at the systematic fabrication of non-persons. The spirit of the old usages seems to be precisely this.

As to the new usages, although slightly simplified, they represent no real or serious improvement. A mature person can handle the situation fairly well, but it seems to damage the young ones, sometimes quite badly. Perhaps it would not do so if they all came from a stable and secure Catholic environment, but their background is often so ambiguous! As for the supposed security that the Rule seems to promise, this promise cannot be kept if certain basic problems are left unresolved: especially the human and social problems of the insecure American teenager.

August 29

This afternoon I worked on abstract calligraphic drawings. Perhaps I did too many. Some of them seem fairly good. I took a batch into the Frame House last Thursday with Ulfert Wilke and he was a big help in showing how they should be framed.

Afterwards we had lunch and went out to his studio in a garage next to a gambling club. He had some fascinatingly calm large abstractions which I cannot describe. A calligraphic economy of points and small white figures on large black or maroon backgrounds. Some lively red and yellow ones, but the somber ones were more serious and profound.

I have not done much writing except letters for the last two weeks. I have to get back to writing next week. I am doing footnotes as an afterthought for the pilgrimage-crusade article. I also had to change the "Monk in the Diaspora" for the French translation. The Abbot General does not like it.

September 1

St. Giles. I said the Mass of St. Giles in a lovely starlit pre-dawn. Cool and silent. The old moon and the liquid silver morning star shining in the sky; and now it is a clear September day, warm and bright. One feels that the year has definitely turned and is moving toward the fall.

*   *   *

There are some very moving passages and sentences in the Meriol Trevor biography of Newman that is being read in the refectory, particularly prayers and lines from his journal. I feel closer and closer to Newman, yet with an ever deeper respect for his religious depth.

It has been a busy day. After Chapter, there was a council meeting and then I had to go and talk with the Cuban family brother, who had become psychotic. He was shouting and breaking dishes and pounding on the walls. He said that the wrath of God was coming down on this place because it was too rich and why does there have to be so much *cleaning* in the guesthouse? He pronounced the word *limpieza* with infuriated precision. I suppose that long hours of work, left to himself, together with his inability to talk English and his intense meditations on the threats and promises of Our Lady of Fatima, on the Apocalypse and on Castro, had finally cracked him up. He tried to demonstrate to me how in Roman numerals the apocalyptic number 666 spelled out the name of Fidel Castro Ruiz, but I was not able to see this. He is leaving today and will go to a place where there are other Cubans.

*   *   *

In the middle of the morning, as I was getting down to type footnotes for "Pilgrimage and Crusade," the X— family from Jackson, Mississippi, arrived. She is a convert who has been writing to me for quite a while and he is still an Episcopalian minister. It is a lovely family. We talked for an hour or so and I got some idea of the difficulty of the moderate Southerner who wants to do what is right and who is caught in the grip of totalism and prejudice so that the slightest misstep puts him out of touch with his neighbors. Yet he does not know who to trust among the outsiders. It is a very difficult position and they really mean well. They have a lot of courage.

September 4

José, the Cuban, has stayed here a few more days and today I spoke to the priest who is taking him to his boys' home in Covington. José is apparently better since we decided he must leave. The priest said there were four days of race riots in Philadelphia, the worst ones yet. Worse than Harlem and Rochester. I don't know any details.

* * *

Yesterday Father Abbot gave me several pages of notes, proposals for the abbots' meeting in October. The notes are extracted from letters of the participants, indicating points they think important and want to discuss. Theoretical and rather useless points attacking the ideas of Jacques and Raïssa Maritain on liturgy of several years ago. Vehement pleas for a vernacular liturgy, a very testy demand for immediate action and "an end to gradualism in dealing with the brothers," as if the question of the Cistercian lay brothers were identical with that of civil rights. The one who wrote it insinuated that "certain abbots" wanted to keep the brothers as a reservoir of "slave labor."

In actual fact, at least here, many of the brothers want to keep their status as a guarantee of a certain amount of *freedom* to be left to themselves and not forced to go to choir or fitted into a mold designed for them by somebody else! I am rather depressed by all these notes, which bear witness to a style of life and to aspirations in which I have no real interest, a form of monasticism in which solitude and contemplation are treated as if they were more or less irrelevant. These people evidently think all that matters is a lively and interesting choral service, well-organized work, a big lively, booming, swinging community. And so forth!

September 10

For the third time this summer, an allergy has taken the skin off my forefingers and thumbs and it seems to be spreading farther. I have a little of it on my face.

*　　*　　*

Czeslaw Milosz was here yesterday. The same face as on his new French book, but considerably older. I am quite enthusiastic about the Polish poets that he has gathered into an anthology which is to be published by Doubleday. There is a great deal of irony, depth and sophistication, intelligence and passion in these wonderful new poets. It all seems to me to be very real, very human. I react to it as I do to most new Latin American verse, as to something which belongs to my world. I can hardly say this for most American or English poetry, except people like Stevie Smith and Peter Levi.

*　　*　　*

Abraham Heschel has sent me a memo on the new Jewish Chapter at the Vatican Council. The new proposal is incredibly bad. All the meaning has been taken out of it. All the originality, all the light are gone and it has become a stuffy, pointless piece of formalism with the stupid addition that the Church is looking forward with hope to the union of the Jews with herself. As a humble, theological, eschatological desire, yes, maybe, but that is not what was meant.

This lack of spiritual and eschatological sense, this unawareness of the real need for profound change, is what makes such statements pitiable. One feels a total lack of prophetic insight and even of elementary compunction. Where is the prophetic and therefore deeply humiliated and humanly impoverished thirst for light, that Christians and Jews may begin to find some kind of unity in seeking God's will together? But if Rome simply declares herself complacently to be the mouthpiece of God and perfect interpreter of God's will for the Jews, with the implication that He in no way ever speaks to them directly, this is simply monstrous! It is perfectly true that the Church, in the highest sense, can indeed speak a message of prophecy and salvation to the Jews, but to say that the juridical niceties of curial officials and well-meaning Council fathers are *the only source of light* for the Jews today would be a fantastic misunderstanding of the Church's true mission! Reflect that the Church in this rather imperfect sense, this exterior sense, delivered the Jews over to Hitler without a murmur, here and there helping a few individuals to escape to make it less intolerable to conscience!

September 12
This is everything that a September day ought to be. Brilliant blue sky, kind sun, cool wind in the pines. But I have to wear white dermal gloves. I am afraid my skin condition is due to poison ivy in the woods. I seem to have become extraordinarily sensitive to *something*. Whatever I do, my skin breaks out more and more, even on my face. Fortunately, I can go with my face bare. I would hate to have to go around with a mask looking like a Ku Kluxer.

*   *   *

Tiny delicate fishbones of clouds in the sky. Harps of sound in the sweet trees, long shadows on the grass. The distant bottomland is flat, level and brown; plowed and harrowed.

*   *   *

Last night on a night watch, I stopped in the library and read about the discoveries of Olduvai in the *National Geographic*. The whole story is inspiring. I find it most religiously stirring. Six hundred thousand years ago, there was this man evolving and making tools out of pebbles and he was strong, he was bigger than I. He lived in great African rains and there were glaciers in the north and south. There were pigs as big as rhinos. What wonderful stories. More fabulous than the fables of the old days. Myth, tradition, racial memories and truth in them. Dragons, for instance. I wonder how many of our familiar stories that we heard as children go back all the way to Olduvai.

*   *   *

Yesterday a long letter came from the Abbot General saying in effect, "If you have such a lot of new ideas, tell me what they are."

Well, I wrote at once some three pages on monastic changes and suggested a committee to study the formation of an American hermitage. This will probably meet all kinds of opposition. Perhaps, first of all, from Dom James. I do not expect to get anywhere with it, but why not at least bring the subject up. If they want to know what I am thinking, now they know. All this started with the article "The Monk in the Diaspora," which turns out after all to have been a kind of time bomb. I heard from Brother Pachomius of Erlach about it today. He likes it and is translating it into German.

*   *   *

The censor of the order at New Melleray, Father Shane Regan, says that I am "written out," that I know no theology or philosophy, that I have nothing to say, and that I ought to stop publishing, but he grants the *nihil obstat* to *Seasons of Celebration*.

*   *   *

Dom James in Chapter today voiced the highest praise for those who simply "run with the herd." These are his own words. He extolled those who do not think for themselves but conform. He regrets that "conformism" is regarded as a bad trait by those who seek "only liberty to do their own will."

He wonders why he has problems with so many monks leaving! So, I am supposed to give a magic talk to the abbots' meeting to dissect the mind of youth and to show where all their trouble comes from! I honestly think that he expects me to say in some way or other that all the troubles of youth come from radicalism, rebellion and self-will. This is the only answer he is prepared to believe.

September 13

Sunday morning was bright, windy and fresh. One of the novices saw smoke to the north before Prime and he and I and Brother Colman drove up to see where it came from. It was on Andy Boone's land. Brush was burning on a hillside in a little pine grove. Andy had just set it alight and left it. A small pine tree was on fire, but it did not seem that the fire was going anywhere. We went to the farmhouse and then to the barn. I had never been to that house before. A little orange-colored puppy came running out in the grass in silence. Lovely Sunday silence and peace over everything. Vistas of the shining and blessed hills of the clean quiet valley. Hills and woods. Small houses looking wiser and safer for the Lord's day. Andy, shaved and at peace after Mass, was bringing in some fodder for his cows. It was his sixty-second birthday.

I missed Chapter and was not sorry to have done so because the Sunday Chapters are awful.

September 15

Hot, very bright, the skin is off my hands. I have various medicines but they don't work. Father Eudes promised he was going to get me Rhulicream ten days ago but nothing happened.

*   *   *

Mother Luke from Loretto was here for a talk before going to Rome. The Third Session of the Council opened yesterday. She will consult with Cardinal Suenens and he is trying to arrange some way in which nuns can be represented on the sacred congregations.

*   *   *

I am writing some notes on Flannery O'Connor, who died this summer.

September 19

Yesterday in rain, I went to town to see old Dr. Simon, the allergist, who said something about "fungus infection." Surely that can hardly account for the state that my hands have been in for three weeks. They are somewhat better, but being in the woods seems to affect them. Perhaps, however, I am mistaken about poison ivy. Maybe I am affected by something that goes along with oak wilt. Maybe I have the disease of some tree!

It was pleasant driving to town in the rain, getting there in the rain, sitting in the doctor's office stripped to the waist with the patch tests itching on my back, watching the rain come down on the bus station, the *Courier-Journal* building and the post office. I was there ten years ago, when I had bad sinus and more colds. The doctor seemed old and prim and the room I was in was full of faded manila folders, shelves of them, records of patients probably going back thirty years or more.

He gave me a good ointment, some wild-looking pills and a serum for shots.

September 22

More rain today. Semi-tropical heat, dampness, haze, the kind of mist that sours and rasps in your throat. But I had a good day at the hermitage. I was reading some notes that Father Tarcisius had brought back from Rome.

Father Prior wrote me a note yesterday with some ideas on the hermit life. There is no question that this remains a live and urgent issue. No amount of official stifling will ever completely smother it. There are too many genuine vocations coming here, people who will never be fully content merely with the formal and official pattern of common life. There is no question, once again, that I am only fully normal and human when I have plenty of solitude. Not that I think a great deal when I am alone, but I live according to a different and more real tempo. I live with the tempo of the sun and of the day, in complete harmony with what is all around me.

It would be infidelity to deny or evade the obvious truth that, for me, such a life is completely and fully right. I cannot doubt it was the life I was meant for. Most of my troubles come from my tendencies to half believe those who doubt it. But I have got to the point where I can no longer take them seriously. Obviously, I am still limited by my obedience. The question tends to answer itself by itself because I am more and more alone, and solitude ceases to become a problem and gradually becomes a fact.

Whether others like or approve does not concern me much anymore. From the moment that I have the permissions and approvals that are required; and I have these or enough of them to make a difference!

* * *

A news report read today with incredible unction in the refectory says that on the opening workday of the Council, the fathers got off to a fast start which resolved itself into a long schoolmarmish warning by Pericle Felici (the dean of discipline). The fathers must not try to go to the coffee bar before 11 a.m. and if they go they will find it closed. Furthermore, it will be no good for them to knock on the door. He then darkly threatened theologians and others who might feel tempted to pass out handbills in the neighborhood of St. Peter's. There was a row about this last year and Felici was photographed snatching handbills from a bishop who was giving them out on the steps of St. Peter's.

September 24
I drove with Brother Nicholas into the hills behind New Hope where Everett Edelin has some land which he may leave to the monastery. A perfect remote, silent, enclosed valley about two miles deep, thickly wooded, watered by a spring and a creek, no roads, perfect solitude, where there were once two cabins for freed slaves a hundred years ago. Now it is all cattle. A herd of three hundred heifers and Angus roaming loose in the pasture and the woods with at least two full-grown, thoroughbred black Angus bulls, not to mention scores of bull calves. They were quiet though.

The silence, the woods and the hills were perfect. This will be an ideal place for some hermitages. One could run a road up through the woods, bypassing New Hope and far from the county road, and have a house and chapel for people coming up for a few days. Then scatter five or six hermitages on the hillside for permanent occupants. It could be marvelous. I am anxious to get this project studied if Dom James will let his suspicion be allayed and his inertia be moved.

September 25
This Ember Week has been quite fantastic, alive, full of unexpected things. Brilliant days and surprises and absurd hopes that

yet seem astonishingly firm. It suddenly seems to be a week of *kairos*. Yesterday (after many doubts and hesitations) I spoke to Father Abbot about the project of hermitages in Edelin's valley and suddenly found him remarkably interested and open. I was astonished! He seemed to take the project really seriously!

He listened to everything I said, raised good questions, had constructive comments to offer and was thoroughly ready to get in it. This was marvelous. I actually think there is a very real possibility that this will go through. It is certainly something to work for. And now I look with astonishment across the valley at those hills. Trees hide the ridge behind which the valley is hidden but I am aware of those silences with a new sense of meaning.

*　　*　　*

Yesterday I went to the mailbox and there was a letter from Father Dumoulin in Tokyo saying that I ought to come to Japan for a few months to get firsthand knowledge of Zen. He thought it was very important and had spoken about it to one of the bishops and to a Trappist superior and they were all willing to have me there. There was nothing else to do but propose this to Dom James, but he was completely shocked by it. He does not seem at all disposed to give me this permission but added that he would study the question objectively with the Abbot General. I'm sure his mind is completely against it. He agreed that it was reasonable, but I can see that he retains all his objections.

September 28
Continuous rain yesterday and today. Box scores of Council voting are read out in the refectory. The collegiality of bishops got through by an immense majority. The debating on whether Mary ought to be called Mother of the Church did not seem to be very relevant, at least from the news reports. Hostile editorials from papers in Israel criticize the revised Jewish Chapter and were quoted in a news article. The Jewish issue is just not understood at all.

*　　*　　*

I have not yet written out my notes for the talk I am supposed to give the abbots next Monday at their meeting here. I must also try to draw up a list of observances that seem to have become useless and ought to be changed. I wonder if this makes too much sense, however. One can lose a sane perspective by focusing on one little observance after another and say "this is not meaningful." From a certain viewpoint, each one may retain a meaning.

The issue of the brothers is, monastically speaking, most important. The brothers have an authentic and simple monastic life. One of the best forms in the Church. They are left pretty much on their own, with a lot of responsibility and good work to do. People want to take this from them and herd them into choir. Actually, as long as it is a question of one category of monks, there is no problem. The real problem comes if the two kinds of life are radically changed.

Looking through the "Usages" for things that might be dropped as artificial, I notice with alarm that they are all built into the very structure of the life. To take away these observances would in fact be to take away what practically constitutes the "Trappist life" for many of the older monks. This is then quite serious.

Is there any real adaptation possible without a complete change of everything? Does that mean that all that can be expected is to preserve what we have and try to keep alive a certain reasonable and alert spirit in community and be at peace away from all of this when one is free? It is a problem, probably more easily accepted in French monasteries.

October 2

Dark, wet, warm. Continuous throbbing of guns at Fort Knox. For the last three days I have been working hard on material for the talk to the abbots' meeting next Monday. I dread that week of talking. I must have written over seven thousand words and set them aside as too long and too complex.

Then I attacked the whole thing over again from another angle, about two thousand five hundred words perhaps. All in notes, not yet saying what I really want to say. Perhaps it is not yet what ought to be said at all. Perhaps, too, my own feelings and frustrations are too much involved. However, I will try to be objective and peaceful in giving it all out.

Meanwhile, I feel a great deal of inner tension, a deep, frantic, knotted anguish of helplessness in the center of me somewhere, as if the whole thing were a complete waste of time that has to be gone through without reason.

And yet yesterday Dom James was very positive, very eager and very encouraging, talking about the hermitage plan, concerning which I gave him a long memorandum Wednesday morning. He himself has been over to see the valley and wants the plan to go through. He says he is convinced it is from God and wants to talk of practical details. In fact, we had a very good conversation. This is very encouraging and consoling from a certain point of view.

And yet there are some anxieties still in it for me, as I don't want to be too closely associated with him in it. There is so much in him that I cannot accept or understand. Not in his reticences and suspicions so much as in his sweeping and at times almost inhuman bursts of idealism—that which he keeps most to himself. Yet he seems in a way to live by it. Nevertheless, one thing is sure, when he gets his mind set on something like this, a foundation or a new project, he usually has his way. He knows how to handle the politics of it better than anyone. (This was the actual beginning of my own permission to live all the time in the hermitage, because he began to take this thing seriously and positively. I got permission to sleep in the hermitage a few months later and permission to live there all the time the following year. As far as I'm concerned, that was the *kairos* that was involved in that week in September of that year.)

October 8

We are in the middle of the meeting of abbots and novice masters and I am exhausted. I have had to talk too much. It goes on all day. Yesterday I got to no Office except None. Sessions began at 7 a.m. and went on practically until dinner. We talked all during dinner. After dinner I got away and sat in the sun and tried to read but could hardly get my mind on the book. The weather is beautiful. How nice it must be in the woods!

Today it was (naturally) proposed that the novice masters have further meetings, but if I never go to any more, it won't worry me. Yesterday's meeting about the future of the brothers was important and lively and in spite of Dom C—'s crusading approach, it seems to be an earnest effort in the right direction. It is really wrong to speak of abolishing the brothers, though the nature of their life will probably be to some extent changed, but so will the life of everybody be changed. Certainly it would be preposterous merely to move the brothers en masse into the choir. At Spencer, as here, a great number of professed brothers are opposed to changes, not quite knowing what to expect.

The meeting of novice masters takes place separately from the abbots after the coffee break. Our meetings are much more peaceful and more academic than theirs—and probably mean nothing.

October 12

The meeting ended three days ago and I am still rocking with the trauma of it. Continual talk. I kept myself keyed up with black coffee and so found myself with more and more to say. In the end, I talked too much, as I usually do.

The worst days were the last. As to what was accomplished, I don't know. Certainly there were some gains and it was useful to get to know the various abbots and to understand something about their thinking.

Though the abbots, in general, seemed disposed to favor a little more solitude perhaps in the sense of days of recollection alone and retreats alone, it does not seem likely that the kind of hermitage project such as Dom James was interested in two weeks ago when I proposed it would be completely acceptable. That is to say, a proposal for a laura or a group of hermitages in the valley. It would seem that the superiors of the order would be frightened of this, as a change in the essentials of Cistercian life.

October 13

One good result of the change in the thinking on the part of Dom James since he became interested in the hermitage project and expressed a desire to participate in it himself is that he has given me permission to sleep at my own hermitage once in a while, without any special restriction or further permissions. The understanding is that I can spend the night at the hermitage whenever I want to. Last night I did this for the first time and it was a blessing. It finally helped me to get the noise and agitation of the abbots' meeting out of my system. Though it had been quite cold for several days, I got enough sun into the place in the afternoon to dry it out and warm it up a bit. I got up there about nightfall. Wonderful silence. I said Compline quietly and slowly, with a candle burning before the icon of Our Lady. A deep sense of peace and truth, a realization that this was the way that things are supposed to be, that I was in my right mind for a change. Around the community, I am seldom in my right mind. I slept wonderfully well even though there was a great pandemonium of dogs in the woods when I got up briefly after midnight. I thought I would hear the bell for vigils at the monastery but I did not. However, I woke up soon after that, lit the fire, and said Lauds quietly, slowly and thoughtfully, sitting on the floor.

October 16

Today I was supposed to go to the doctor about the skin that is broken out again on my hands. I had an appointment and I had also arranged to say Mass in Carmel, but Father Abbot told me instead that I was to meet the Mayor of Florence, Giorgio La Pira, at the Louisville airport, so I went there after Carmel. He was there with the head of his school board, a reporter and a young physicist, on a quick official visit to the U.S. Full of ebullient and strong statements about everything from NASA to Gethsemani and declaring that "the Council ought to canonize John XXIII by acclamation."

There was a considerable mix-up at the airport, but I finally found him and his companions. We talked volubly in French in the airport, blocking traffic in all directions. Continued in the car coming out. Talked about the Council, about his trip to Moscow, to Africa. We talked less volubly, still in French, during dinner with Dom James, at which Dubonnet was served as a wine. After dinner my volubility was entirely gone but his was still in high gear. I showed them the novitiate and the refectory, etc. I was left at last with a strong impression of the meaning and greatness of Florence; and of his *spes contra spem* (hope against hope) and the reality of his convictions and of his mission. As I left him, he was writing out a telegram to Pope Paul, hailing him from Gethsemani with the assurance of prayers.

After I left, I got on the phone to Dr. Scheen, whom I will see next week. The hands are getting better anyway.

October 19

I am reading some interesting texts from an Ethiopian monastic collection, a late manuscript which is very traditional and full of meat. Also, von Balthasar's book *Word and Revelation* is excellent. In one fine passage he says substantially what Julian of Norwich says about "all manner of things shall be well," namely: that Christ judges and separates good from evil in order to reveal the truth about man in this separation; but the rejected will turn out to have been those chosen with a greater and more mysterious mercy. Can there be a limit to the mercy of Christ who has *fully satisfied forever* all God's justice and now has the world in his hand to do with according to his merciful love?

In spite of all this about love and mercy, nevertheless, yesterday I was angry as assistant priest standing next to the abbot at the altar. Clearly it is my pride. A real distraction and a threat to faith. But when I think of the power that authority has to be most unreasonable in our lives, and see how that power is sometimes used so arbitrarily, I am filled with frustration and resentment. Yet it is precisely this that I must accept. This should be all the easier when he has, in fact perhaps also unreasonably, given me so much latitude in other matters.

October 20

Yesterday afternoon, the Abbot of Spencer stopped here on his way back east from the new foundation of nuns he has just made in Iowa. There was some discussion of two points he will bring up at the meeting of abbots before the General Chapter.

One regards the lay brothers and the other regards the solitude in the order.

About the second question, I wrote to the Abbot General last Sunday.

Whether the order will officially recognize the eremitical life as appropriate for Cistercians and as permissible within the order is not at all certain, but it is possible that a relative solitude such as I already have may be recognized and permitted in some form or other.

At the same time I am beginning to see that the question of solitude for me is finally getting to be no longer a question of desire but of decision. I still do not know what scope for decision may be given me, but I do know that I must prepare to face a serious decision and one about which I had more or less given up thinking and hoping. It seems to be a real "encounter with the Word" that I must not evade. Yet as in all such things, I am not too sure just where the encounter is except that my heart tells me that in this question of the solitary life there is for me a special truth to be embraced. A truth which is not capable of fully logical explanation. A truth which is not rooted in my own nature or in my own biography, but is something deeper and something that may also cut clean through the whole network of my own recent works, ideas, writing, experiences and so forth—even those that in some way concern the solitary life and monastic renewal.

For the moment, this encounter seems to involve also cutting off a hundred contacts in the world and even legitimate and fruitful concerns with the events and needs of the time. I do not yet know or understand how far this has to go, except that I am caught in all kinds of affairs that are no longer my business. Then they prove to be evasions and distraction. I do not yet see where to begin breaking off contact and I do not trust the judgments of others in this regard. I am sure the decision finally has to be my own. Also the decision will have to involve renouncing finally some of the securities of community life. Sleeping in the hermitage is a great grace and I sleep well.

Last night there was a full moon. At midnight the whole valley was drenched in silence and dark clarity.

It was cold this morning. Going down to the monastery in the dark, I could feel frost on the grass and on the dry corn husks under my feet.

October 21
Lamplight! It is good, quiet. Many years since I have had a lamp to read by. Not since France forty years ago.
The lamp came today. It was in a paper bag on my desk in the novitiate after High Mass.

October 25, Twenty-third Sunday after Pentecost
On Thursday I was in town and saw the skin doctor. Things are slowly improving but this trouble with this skin on my hands is a great mystery of pollen and wavelengths of light, something more than I am capable of understanding.
I went to Catherine Spalding College with the twenty-six abstract drawings of mine that are to be exhibited there in November. They are well framed, thanks to Ulfert Wilke's advice. They look pretty good, at least to me. I gave them names and prices not without guilt feelings. (Am I perpetuating a hoax?) But the drawings themselves, I think, are very good with or without names and prices. Wilke says, "They are real."

*   *   *

Yesterday Marco Pallis was here. He is touring with his English Consort of Viols. I was glad to meet him.
I would have liked to hear the viols play some Orlando Gibbons, but this was not possible. We spoke of Zen and of Shin and of Tibetan Buddhism and how if Tibetans were to seek refuge out of India it would probably be in America rather than Japan, though Japan is Buddhist. And why? Because of the ease and simplicity with which they become totally infatuated with the West.

October 29
Clouds running across the face of the waning moon. Distant flashes of lightning. It is a "warm front," etc. Clouds running over

the face of the waning moon, and who cares what the official weather may be? It is money that cares about weather and pays to predict it, perhaps someday to control it. But who wants a world in which weather is controlled by money?

*　　*　　*

Last night I slept in the monastery, because direction ran late in the novitiate and my shoulder was hurting; I wanted the traction which is fixed up on my bed in the novitiate dormitory. Sleeping in the hermitage gives one a totally different sense of time—measured by the phases of the moon (whether or not one will need a flashlight), etc. This in itself is important. The whole day has different dimensions.

As for Office in choir, its artificiality impresses me more and more. Not that it is not a good thing, not that there is not a great will to do good and praise God there, but the whole decor of habits and stalls and stained glass seems unreal when you have been praying the Psalms among the pine trees.

The thing I most appreciate about the monastery is the electric light. The lamplight of the hermitage is primitive and mysterious, but the lamp smokes and one cannot read well by it. That is all right, since it means more meditation. Yet I like and need to sit here (in the novitiate) with the book open and really read, take notes and study.

As to the brethren, it is good to be with them, to see them (even though I know them enough to recognize their tensions and troubles). But I can tell that a feeling of loneliness for them would probably be a deception or a reflex.

One can love them and still live apart from them without explanation.

*　　*　　*

Yesterday a small deer fell into the reservoir by the new waterworks and thrashed around trying to climb out. But the concrete wall was not negotiable. I was afraid it might drown, but it squeezed through the narrow joists of the footbridge and to the other end, where there was a foothold, and trotted off across the road into the woods, looking beat and confused.

* * *

I rewrote "Monastic Vocation and Modern Thought." Perhaps I am too much concerned with it. In the end I saw it was getting too complicated and I was trying to deepen it so as to avoid merely repeating platitudes about "identity crisis" and "authenticity." Not successful.

* * *

Good news! The abbot has had a letter from the Abbot General saying that he is not opposed on principle to experiments with the hermit life within our order, and that such an experiment on the property of our monastery is quite feasible. He thinks Gethsemani would be a reasonable place for such an experiment. He will discuss it at the December meeting of abbots and it will then be taken up at the General Chapter.

October 30
For three days they have been reading in the refectory a bulletin of the liturgical commission and the congregation of rites on the new changes to go into effect next Lent. The changes are good in the main and are the ones that have been expected. But while they tend to simplicity, the document itself is very complicated, tedious, a ponderous and grim effort to organize everything. To leave nothing unforeseen, even that which seems to be a concession to initiative. How can we have renewal with such elaborate, pompous formalities as this?

* * *

I am reading Jacques Ellul's book on the technological society. Great. Full of firecrackers. A fine, provocative, though pessimistic book. It makes sense. It is good to read this while the Council is busy with Schema 13, as it is now. One cannot see what is involved in the question of the Church and the modern world without at least taking into account the charges of a book like this. I wonder if the fathers are really aware of all the implications of a technological society. Those who can only resist it may be wrong but those who want to go along with all its intemperances are hardly right. Or do they know that this might be what they are really wanting?

*   *   *

Gentle whistle of a bluebird and in the mist a SAC plane swoops huge and low over the ridges where Edelin's valley is and where the final hermitages are supposed to be one day. I wonder if that plane carries bombs. Most probably. They all do, I am told.

Technological society!

I will go out and split some logs and gather a basket of pine cones. Good for starting fires in the small hours of the morning.

October 31

At the hermitage these cold nights I have spontaneously been remembering the days when I first came to Gethsemani twenty-three years ago. The stars, the cold, the smell of night, the wonder (the abandonment, which is something else again than despondency), and above all, the melody of the *Rorate coeli*.

That entire first Advent bore in it all the stamp of my vocation's peculiar character. The solitude, inhabited and pervaded by cold and mystery, by woods and Latin. It is surprising how far we have got from the cold and the woods and the stars since those early days!

My fiftieth year is ending. If I am not ripe for solitude now, I never will be.

This is the *kairos*, say the stars, says Orion, says Aldebaran, says the sickle moon rising behind the dark tall cedar cross. And I remember the words I said to Father Philotheus, which may have been in part a cliché but they were very sincere and I knew at the time that I really meant them and they were unpremeditated. I said, "I want to give God everything." Until now, I really have not. Or perhaps, in a way, I have tried to, but certainly not hard enough.

I cannot say my life in the monastery has been useless or a failure, nor can I say where or how it has really had any meaning, nor will I probably find where and how the hermitage has a meaning. It is enough that there is in the hermitage the same mixture of anguish and certitude, the same sense of walking on water, as when I first came to the monastery.

November 2, All Souls' Day
There was sunlight and haze for the procession in the cemetery. Brother Ephrem was taking photographs of the monks over the wall with a ladder. And as the procession rounded the corners of the cloister, I thought it looked spiritless, as if the monks were going through it all merely with resignation. They were tired from the long Office.

*   *   *

I am going on with Ellul's prophetic and I think very sound diagnosis of technological society.

Certainly he sees the dark side, but how few people really face this problem. It is the most portentous and apocalyptic thing of all. That we are caught in an automatic, self-determining system in which man's choices have largely ceased to count. The existentialist freedom in a void seems to imply a despairing recognition of this plight, but it says and does nothing.

*   *   *

Birds. A titmouse was swinging and playing in the dry weeds by the monastery woodshed. A beautiful, small, trim being. A quail was whistling in the field by the hermitage in the afternoon. What a pure and lovely sound. The sound of perfect innocence.

A tiny shrew was clinging to the inside of the novitiate screen doors, trapped in the house! I took her up and she ran a little onto my sleeve and then stayed fixed, trembling. I put her down in the grass outside and she ran away free.

But what of the wasp in the hermitage that I killed with insecticide? I was shocked to find it an hour later in great agony. It would have been simple and less cruel to have killed it with a flyswatter.

*   *   *

Last night in bed here at the hermitage, I fell asleep thinking of the Aveyron at Bruniquel. There is no longer any train now. I remember all those little stations.

Father Chrysogonus went to Saint-Antonin and wrote me a long letter about it. About the house Father built, which now belongs to a winemaker, and so forth.

Victor Hammer finally wrote. I had been worrying about his health. He tires easily but is working. The operations on his eyes were successful and he can see well, he says.

November 3

Four o'clock. I went out on the porch to see the starlight. The cocks were crowing at Andy Boone's near at hand and then up the road and then off in the east and south, where I did not know they were close enough to be heard.

The bell for Lauds of the feast of St. Malachy had just rung briefly at the monastery. I had just been reading chapters 3 and 4 of Ezechiel: "Thou shalt bear the iniquity of the house of Israel."

During meditation, looking at the fire, I suddenly remembered, this was Election Day.

November 4

Yesterday before dawn, I wrote a four-line Latin poem at Victor Hammer's request. A thanksgiving for the return of his sight so that he works again and he wants this for an inscription.

One thing saddens and embarrasses me. Victor will be shocked at my exhibition of drawings or calligraphies or whatever you want to call them. There is no way to explain this to him, and in a way, I am on his side on principle. And yet they do have a meaning and there is a reason for them. An unreason reason, perhaps. One which is not understandable to a traditionalist. I feel like writing to him and saying: If you heard I had taken a mistress, you would be sad but you would understand. These drawings are perhaps worse than that, but regard them as a human folly. Allow me, like everyone else, at least one abominable vice, etc.

*   *   *

I went over to vote yesterday just when all the children were coming to school. There was no one at the polls. I ended up voting for Chelf when I did not mean to. I pulled the party lever by mistake and got the whole tribe!

*   *   *

In the afternoon, there were lots of pretty little myrtle warblers playing and diving for insects in the low pine branches over my head. So close, I could almost touch them. I was awed at their loveliness, their quick flight, their lookings and chirpings, the yellow spot on the back revealed in flight. A sense of total kinship with them as if they and I were all of the same nature and as if that nature were nothing but love.

Indeed, what else but love keeps us all together in being?

*   *   *

I am more and more convinced that Romans 9–11 (the chapters on the election of Israel) are *the key to everything today*. This is the point where we have to look and press and search and listen to the word. From here we enter the understanding of Scripture, the wholeness of Revelation and of the Church.

Vatican II is still short of this awareness, it seems to me. The Chapter on the Jews has been woefully inadequate. It was naturally cautious, I will not say to the point of infidelity, but it was certainly obtuse. It got nowhere and in its inadequacy, it is itself a providential sign. A "word." So we must look harder and press further into this mystery.

A contemplation that ignores this, that is wide of this, is simply a waste of time, vanity and vexation of spirit.

November 6

The other morning before Prime, there was a notice in the little cloister saying Johnson had won the Presidential election in a landslide.

After that, I went to Louisville to see the skin doctor again, after which I bought a Coleman lamp and stove. I got the stove filled and working yesterday and the lamp this evening. It gives brighter and better light to read by for longer periods than the kerosene lamp does.

*   *   *

I think Ellul is perhaps *too* pessimistic. There are reasons for it: but one must still have some hope! Perhaps the self-determining course of technology is not as inexorably headed for the end as he imagines. Yet certainly he is logical. But more is involved, thank heaven, than logic! Even though everything may be brought into line to "serve the universal effort" of continual technological development and expansion, even though there may be no place for the solitary, even though no man will be able to disengage himself from society—there will be something else. I do not personally believe that it will end like that. And should I complain of technology with this hissing bright green light, with its comforts and its dangers, or with the powerful flashlight I got at Sears that sends a bright hard pole of light probing deep into the wet forest?

*   *   *

Tonight the new moon was shining in the west; and really *new*. Although men have seen the same moon for more than a million years. That is one of the good things about being in the woods, living by the sun, moon and stars, and gladly using the moonlight, which should now be available for some three weeks on clear nights at the beginning or at the end.

I am surprised how easy it is to follow a familiar path even by starlight alone.

November 7

The Presidential election campaign was hot and dirty. One of the disturbing things about it was the quasi-religious character of the zeal for Goldwater. I am surprised he did not get more votes. For many people, apparently, Goldwaterism was Christianity, and I don't think we have done with this mania.

*   *   *

Reading Ezechiel 6. This is about our idolatry as well as Israel's. Idolatry is the basic sin, therefore, that which is deepest in us, most closely related to Original Sin—therefore, most likely to deceive us under the appearance of true worship or integrity or honesty or loyalty or idealism.

Even Christianity is often idolatrous without realizing it. The sin of having a god who is other than he who cannot be made an idol, i.e., an object.

November 10

This morning I went down to the monastery earlier than usual because I had forgotten my glasses and could not read comfortably in the hermitage. But I was not unaware that it might have been better to meditate in the dark until six rather than read. I settled the case because "I might be needed" in the novitiate.

Nevertheless, the question of using the darkness and limited light in the early hours in the hermitage is not to be ignored. Is this one of the limitations providentially intended for me? Why should I automatically suppose that because it is possible to have electricity and read more, it is therefore necessary to do so? Still, there are other considerations and it was certainly profitable to read von Balthasar and Gordon Zahn's little book on the Austrian conscientious objector Franz Jaegerstaetter, which is surprisingly good and moving. Also, if I had not gone down, I would not have corrected the letter to *Ramparts* on their policy toward Cardinal McIntyre and decided to send it.

*   *   *

Yesterday a large group of baptists from the Southern Baptist Seminary in Louisville were here. I enjoyed talking to them but I do not think I will continue that next year. It is obviously fruitful and meaningful but you can't do everything.

*   *   *

The exhibition of drawings at Catherine Spalding College is to open next Sunday. A private showing will be held on Friday. Already everyone seems very interested in it. Apparently, there was something in the *Courier-Journal* about it, which of course I did not see.

Finally, last Saturday, Monsignor Moore, who instructed and

baptized me twenty-eight years ago this Sunday, was here briefly with Jack Ford from Bellarmine. That was on Saturday afternoon. It was good to see him again. He is not much changed, is a bit fatter and in better health. He has been chaplain at West Point for twenty-five years.

*   *   *

Here is a quotation that needs no comment: "The truth about the nature and risk of thermonuclear war is available. The reason why it is not embraced is that it is not acceptable. People cannot risk being overwhelmed by the anxiety which might accompany a full cognitive and effective grasp of the present world situation and its implications for the future. It serves a man no useful purpose to accept this truth if doing so leads only to very disquieting feelings which interfere with his capacity of productivity to enjoy life and to maintain his mental equilibrium" (*Peace News*, November 6, 1964).

*   *   *

I continue to read proofs of Zahn's book on the Austrian peasant Jaegerstaetter, who was executed by Hitler for his conscientious objection and refusal to fight in the Nazi war. It is an excellent job. Moving above all are the notes of Jaegerstaetter himself, his commentaries on the war. Their lucidity and accuracy is astonishing and so much greater than that of many bishops and scholars and commentators of the time.

Here was a simple, barely educated man who saw things clearly and stated them as he saw them.

One thing strikes me above all. The Catholic Church in Germany and Austria, having condemned Nazism before it came to power and having afterwards collaborated with it when in power, was surely aware that Nazism was irreconcilably opposed to the Church just as much as Communism. Why did the Church support Nazism and never compromise with Communism? Perhaps because the Nazis were more pragmatic in offering a means to compromise. But also basically, the real reason, because of *property*.

November 16

Twenty-sixth anniversary of my baptism.

Warm and dark coming down from the hermitage. Warm wind and stars. Moon nearly full, had set. They have harrowed the corn field in the bottom by the sheep barn and it will be rough to walk through when they shall have plowed it.

*   *   *

Brother Antoninus, tall, bowed, gentle, benevolent, given to quiet laughter, was here from Friday to Sunday. We had some good talks and he spoke to the novices and juniors of the poet's presence, the poet's aura, his tone, his ear, imagination, sovereign intellect, the compassion of images. Antoninus reads poetry more attentively and intelligently than I do.

He told me I was well reviewed by Hayden Carruth in the *Hudson Review*. I had vaguely heard of this but had not seen it.

Brother Antoninus did not like Lowell's new book [*For the Union Dead*]. He was offended by its destructiveness and its desiccation. He did not like Lowell's obsession with destroying that in himself that might save him. But for my part (less compassionate, no doubt), I liked its hardness.

*   *   *

Technology!

No! When it comes to taking sides, I am not with the *Beati* who are openmouthed in awe at the "New Holiness" of a technological cosmos in which man condescends to be God's collaborator and to improve everything for Him. Not that technology is by itself impious or unholy. It is simply neutral and there is no greater nonsense than taking it for an ultimate value. It is *there*; and our love and compassion for other men is now framed and scaffolded by it. Then what?

We gain nothing by surrendering to technology as if it were a ritual, a worship, a liturgy, or talking of our liturgy as if it were an expression of the sacred values supposedly now revealed in technological power. Where impiety begins is in the hypostatizing of mechanical power as something to do with the incarnation as its fulfillment, as its Epiphany.

When it comes to taking sides, I am perhaps with Ellul and also with Massignon rather than with Teilhard de Chardin.

November 17

Abbé Monchanin was convinced of the great importance of his prayer for "all the dead of India" as part of his mission to India, as part of the "convergence" of all mankind upon the Christ of the Day of Judgment.

Massignon and Foucauld were both converted to Christianity by the witness of Islam to the one true living God.

Someone wrote of Foucauld and of his devotion to the dead of Islam. For a mystic the souls of the dead count as much as those of the living, and his particular vocation was to sanctify the eternal Islam—that which has been and will be for eternity—in helping it to give a saint to Christianity.

Massignon says: Asceticism is not a solitary luxury which ornaments us to please God but is the deepest work of mercy, that which heals the hearts broken by its own breaking and wounding.

*　　*　　*

Today an FOR [Fellowship of Reconciliation] group is coming for retreat. A. J. Muste, Jim Forest, John Howard Yoder, Dan and Phil Berrigan, John Oliver Nelson, etc. Paul Peachey cannot come. He had to fly to London at the last moment to replace John Heidbrink, who is having an operation on his spine. Tom Cornell, editor of the *Catholic Worker*, and Tony Walsh from Montreal are also coming with W. H. Ferry.

November 19

The FOR retreat has been remarkably lively and fruitful. Sessions in the gatehouse mostly, because of rain, but we got to the hermitage yesterday afternoon. Ferry has been very helpful. He and I talked a lot at first about Ellul. John Yoder spoke well this afternoon on protest from the Mennonite viewpoint that is Biblical. Relation of technology to the "principalities and powers" of St. Paul. Not at all alien to the mind of Ellul, whom he, in fact, quoted (and whom he knows personally). For personal intensity and sincerity, I also liked very much the remarks of Elbert Jean, a Methodist from the South. He was a minister in Birmingham and was fired for his integrationist ideas. ("Desegregation can be brought about by anyone, but integration only by the Holy Spirit.")

* * *

A. J. Muste is impressive in real wisdom, modesty, gentleness. In a way he reminds me of Archbishop Floersh and yet he is much more mild, free from institutional cramps and compulsions.

Today, as we were beginning our session, Brother Patrick gave me twelve brand-new copies of *Seeds of Destruction* (just out) for the retreatants. *Motive* also came with three of my letters in it.

* * *

Dan Berrigan said a far-out Mass in the novitiate chapel, yet it was beautiful too. We had two ministers, Nelson and Muste, read the gospel and epistle. Dan's celebration of the sacrificial liturgy was simple and impressive. All in English and "uncanonical" even to the extreme point, not only of Communion in both kinds but Communion to the Protestants. I suppose it will be the same again tomorrow in the old juniorate chapel, where the altar is better suited for standing around in a circle.

* * *

Last night I had a haunting dream of a Chinese princess which stayed with me all day. ("Proverb" again.) This lovely and familiar and archetypal person. (No "object" yet how close and real, and how elusive.) She comes to me in various mysterious ways in my dreams. This time she was with her "brothers," and I felt overwhelmingly the freshness, the youth, the wonder, the truth of her; her complete reality, more real than any other, yet unobtainable. Yet I deeply felt the sense of her understanding, knowing and loving me, in my depths—not merely in my individuality and everyday self, yet not as if this self were utterly irrelevant to her. (Not rejected, not accepted either.)

* * *

And now a rainy night. I sit writing this in the green technological light of the Coleman lamp at the hermitage. They will leave
tomorrow.

November 22

After the rain yesterday, Office of the Presentation of Our Lady,
which we still, to my surprise, are celebrating as a feast of sermon.

The weather got cold and bright. Very cold, in fact. It must have
been twenty when I went up to the hermitage to sleep and apparently it was down around five or ten this morning. And now, though
the sun has been up for hours, the grass still shines with thick
frost.

I observed the whiskers of frost on the dead cornstalks and on
the creosoted gateposts. I walked out to the little pond in the ravine
that goes through the knobs to Hanekamp's old place and I walked
about praying Psalms in the dry shaly place on the rise where small
pines are coming back in.

Wasted (perhaps) time and film photographing an old root with
inexhaustibly interesting forms, convolutions and textures in the
weak sun.

*   *   *

No matter how naïve the medieval doctrine of *quies* may seem,
it makes sense. It is part of a whole which we no longer have
(Chartres), but I am nevertheless not divorced from it.

I realized this clearly, singing with attention the Gregorian mel-
odies of the feast. They are simple, solid, incomparable though
only from the common. They are perfectly satisfying, without being
the best in Gregorian.

*   *   *

Always I have the sense that any new Church music we may
attempt will be less good than Gregorian. No adequate replacement.
How in my early days here the chant gave meaning and coherence
to the whole day here for me!

*   *   *

Adam the Carthusian has a fine text on *Quies Claustralis* which has been published by Leclercq. He sums it all up simply and adequately, the need for *quies*: or not bothering with concerns foreign to our life.

I want to give up the retreats. Yet, already a letter has come from the Baptist Seminary begging me not to stop my talks. I was touched by it. No one could be more sincere and less political than Glenn Hinson, who wrote it.

November 24, Feast of St. John of the Cross

In the night, a rumpled thin skin of cloud covered the skies, not totally darkening the moon. It has become thicker as the morning wears on. There is a feeling of snow in the air. Streaks of pale lurid light over the dark hills in the south.

The SAC planes sailed low over the valley just after the bell for Consecration at the conventual Mass and an hour later another one went over even nearer, almost over the monastery. Enormous, perfect, ominous. Great swooping weight, gray, full of her burden of bombs and proud of being "the key to peace."

*   *   *

Today is my full day at the hermitage. No question whatever that this is the kind of schedule to live by. I went down to say Mass and will go down again for dinner. The rest of the time here does not begin to be enough. How full the days are. Full and slow and quiet. Ordered, occupied (sawing wood, sweeping, reading, taking notes, meditating, praying, tending the fire or just looking at the valley).

Only here do I feel that my life is fully human. And only what is authentically human is fit to be offered to God. There is no question in my mind that the artificiality of life in the community is, in its own small way, something quite deadly (saved by the fact that the artificiality of life in the "world" is totally monstrous and irrational).

*   *   *

It is good to know how cold it is and not by looking at the thermometer, to wear heavy clothes and cut logs for the fire.

I like washing in the small basin with the warm water left over from making coffee and then walking down in the moonlight to say Mass with the frozen leaves growling under my feet. Not pulled at, not tense, not waiting for what is to descend on me next, not looking for a place quiet enough to read in.

Life here seems real. In the community it is mental, forced. You can see some of them "thinking." (About what?) And others behind whose frowns there is no place for thought left. Only the tension of being and of forfeiture, all "offered up."

God is doubtless pleased with them or full of compassion for them: but what a system.

November 29

There have been some good rains in the last few days. This morning, with rain pounding down all over everything, I looked out from the novitiate porch over the shining wet roof of the sheep barn and I gave a conference on Péguy's poem about Chartres.

> *Nous ne demandons rien dans ces amendements,*
> *Reine, que de garder, sous vos commandements*
> *Une fidélité plus forte que la mort!*

*　　*　　*

The Council session ended last week. I have not yet read the full reports, but the whole thing seems to have been decidedly ambiguous and disturbing. The Pope overruled a majority of the bishops at the last moment. Not only on the question of liberty of conscience (this has been put off *again*) but on various others. I am not sure exactly what took place but there is anger in the air. Since I do not know exactly what happened, I shall say nothing of it at the moment. At best, there are unpleasant rumors going around.

*　　*　　*

Yesterday I was in Louisville. The skin on my hands is in bad shape. It is "badly damaged" after the long siege of dermatitis.

I was able to see the drawings as they are now hung at Catherine Spalding. A very attractive exhibit.

November 30
I woke up in the hermitage at 2:30 and walked out to see snow on the ground with the wind blowing snowflakes around my bare ankles. I lit the fire and said Lauds. No trouble seeing the way down to the monastery in the dark with all that snow on the ground.

*   *   *

The Christian faith enables or should enable a man to stand back from society and its institutions, to realize that they are all under the inscrutable judgment of God and therefore we can never give an unreserved assent to the policies, the programs and the organizations of men or to official interpretations of the historic process. To do so is idolatry. The same kind of idolatry that was refused by the early martyrs, who would not burn incense to the emperor. The Apostles, on the other hand, by reason of their denunciation and detachment from the world, could sit on twelve thrones judging the twelve tribes, society, even sacred society as they knew it. The Pharisees, identifying themselves completely with a social order, carried out the judgment of God upon that order in the very acts by which they sought to defend it.

The mistaken policies of men contain within themselves the judgment of God upon their society. And when the Church identifies her policies with theirs, she too is judged with them, for she has in this been unfaithful and is not truly the Church. She has yielded to the same secret idolatry of power. The power of the Church, who is not truly the Church if she is really rich and powerful, contains in itself the judgment that "begins at the house of God." Judgment begins with the Church! In order not to see it, we fulminate judgments upon Communism and revolution.

*   *   *

Night. Zero cold. Frozen leaves cracking like glass under my feet on the path through the woods.

*   *   *

The REA men must have been here today seeing about the electric line, but I missed them. I saw only their footprints in the snow. I had to stay down in the monastery to see Father Matthew before None.

*   *   *

The other day a letter came to Dom James from Rome about the Japan project. I had been invited to Japan to visit a Zen monastery, staying also in our own monastery in Japan. Both Dom James and the Abbot General have prohibited this trip to Japan. They say that this "cannot possibly be the will of God for our order." It has "nothing to do with the contemplative life." They have no capacity to understand the meaning of it. It does not matter. Maybe I shall still go someday in spite of everything.

December 1

How clearly I see and experience, this morning, the difference and distance between my own inertia, weakness, sensitivity, stupidity and the love of Christ which instantly pulls all things in me together so that there is no longer any uncertainty or misdirection or lassitude. What a shame and what dishonor to Christ if I let my life be such a mess of trivialities, such silly concerns that are in reality only a mask for despair.

*   *   *

I will not easily forget the thin sickle of the cold moon rising this morning just before dawn when I went down to say Mass. Cold sky. Hard brightness of stars through the pines. Snow and frost. Exultation in the bright darkness of morning.

In the cold Advent, I recapture the lostness and wonder of the first days when I came here twenty-three years ago, abandoned to God, with everything else left behind. I have not felt this for a long time here. The monastery is too warm, too busy, too sociable for that. But breaking off and living to such a great extent in the woods brings me back face to face with the loneliness and poverty of the cold hills and the Kentucky winter. Incomparable. The reality of my own life!

* * *

I finished reading Martin Marty's book *Varieties of Unbelief*, which I am supposed to be reviewing for the *Commonweal*.

* * *

Now snow clouds are coming up in the west and the bones of the hills in the south have snow on them. The trees are picked out sharply like iron bristles against a streak of pale indifferent green sky. The alfalfa field in the bottom is as green as watercress, streaked with snow. The evening is very silent.

The bell for Vespers rang early. There must be Office of the Dead. I will go down and check the ordo and say the Office before Collation. Then I will see Dan Walsh, who is full of all the rumors that go around among the brothers about hermits who are to live in trailers in Edelin's valley and so forth. Dan hears everything and, when he tells it, improves it beyond measure.

December 3, Evening

> *The heart is deceitful above all things.*
> *The heart is deep and full of windings.*
> *The old man is covered up in a thousand wrappings.*
> (Lancelot Andrewes)

True, sad words: and I would not have felt the truth of them so much if I had not had so much solitude these days, with rain coming down on the roof and hiding the valley.

Rain in the night, the murmur of water in the buckets. I cut wood behind the house and enjoy a faint smell of hickory smoke from the chimney while I taste and see that I am deceitful and that most of my troubles are rooted in my own bitterness.

Is this what solitude is for? Then it is good, but I must pray for the strength to bear it. (The heart is deceitful and does not want this, but God is greater than my heart.)

I will acknowledge my faults, O Lord,
Oh who will give scourges to my mind
That they spare not my sins?

December 4

It rained all night and is still raining.

How often in the last years I have thought of death. It has been present to me and I have "understood" and known that I must die. Yet last night, only for a moment, in passing and so to speak without grimness or drama, I momentarily experienced the fact that I, this body, this self, will simply not exist. A flash of the "not-thereness" of being dead. Without fear or grief, without anything. Just *not there*. And this, I suppose, is one of the first tastes of the fruits of solitude. As if the Angel of Death passed along, thinking aloud to himself, doing his business and barely taking note of me, but taking note of me nevertheless. So we recognized one another.

*   *   *

In the hermitage I see how quickly one can fall apart. I talk to myself, I dance around the hermitage, I sing. This is all very well, but it is not serious. It is a manifestation of weakness, of dizziness. And again I feel within this individual self the nearness of disintegration.

(Yet I also realize that this exterior self can fall apart and be reintegrated too. This is like losing dry skin that peels off my hands while the new skin forms underneath.)

And I suddenly remember absurd things. The song that my grandfather had on a record forty-five years ago called "The Whistler and His Dog." Crazy. I went out to the jakes with this idiot song rocking my whole being. Its utterly inane confidence, its gaiety (and it is, in its own way, joyful)! The joy of people who had not yet seen World War II and Auschwitz and the Bomb.

Silly as it was, it had life and juice in it too. The confidence of people walking up and down Broadway in derbies in 1910. They thought they were kings of the earth! Sousa's whole mad band, rocking with this idiot confident joy! The strong shrill whistle of the whistler and the bark at the end, which is what I liked best.

Brave whistler! Brave dog! What a collapse since you whistled and barked to each other!

(As a child I had this whistler who whistled to his dog confused with the one who painted his mother.)

December 5

In the hermitage, one must pray or go to seed. The pretense of prayer will not suffice. Just sitting will not suffice. It has to be real. Yet, what can one do? Solitude puts you with your back to the wall, or your face to it, and this is good. So you pray to learn how to pray!

* * *

The reality of death, Donne's poems and Lancelot Andrewes. Then it becomes very important to remember that the quality of one's night depends on the thoughts of the day. I had a somewhat fearsome night after reading Golding's *The Lord of the Flies*. This is a hangover from my cenobitic after-dinner flight into light reading, which is all right. I do not despise it. I read many good books in the woodshed after dinner down at the monastery. Pasternak, Ellul, and others, Stevie Smith, Françoise Henri on Irish art, Auden's *Enchafèd Flood*, and, last summer, Kenneth Jackson's *Early Celtic Nature Poetry*, and so many others.

Still, the quality of one's nights depends on the sanity of the day. I bring there the sins of the day into the light and darkness of truth to be adored without disguise, then I want to fly back to the disguises.

* * *

Whoever said that the solitary life is one of pretense and deception as if pretense were easy in solitude? It is easy in the community, for one can have the support of a common illusion or a common agreement in forms that take the place of truth. One can pretend in the solitude of an afternoon walk, but the night alone destroys all pretenses. One is reduced to nothing and is compelled to begin laboriously the long return to truth.

*   *   *

Evening. After all that, this afternoon I made myself a cup of coffee strong enough to blow the roof off the hermitage and then as a result got into an orgy of abstract drawing. Most of the drawings were awful, some of them even disturbing, so that now I see that I cannot afford to play with this either in solitude. But perhaps I will do some careful and sane drawings based perhaps on Romanesque sculpture, until I get some better ideas. But not now anyway!

Later I went down to the monastery feeling confused and ashamed but singing Vespers and the Advent hymn was a comfort. I will continue to need some liturgy, certainly the conventual Mass for a long time, and Vespers, generally, and the other hours when I am around the monastery.

*   *   *

Tonight it is cold again and as I came back up in the dark a few small snowflakes were flying in the beam of the flashlight. The end of an oak log was still burning with small flames in the fireplace. On the way up, I had been thinking of the letter from one of the novices who left and how he visited the Little Sisters in Chicago and thought maybe of sending them some cheese for Christmas. One of the sisters, he says, seems lonely for her home in France.

I came up with candles and with sugar for coffee. What greater comfort could a man want? Well, of course, I will be glad to get electric light. The question of light is an important one. Not that I have anything against sister lamp here, chaste, quiet and faithful as she is; but she is a bit dim for serious reading. And yet, for centuries, no one had any more than this. St. Thomas Aquinas may have had much less good a light than my lamp here. What am I complaining about?

December 7

In solitude everything has its weight for good or for evil and one must attend carefully to everything. If you apply yourself carefully to what you do, great springs of strength and truth are released in you. If you drift or go inattentively, automatic and obsessed, the strength turns against you and becomes a storm of confusion. It dashes you on the rocks. And when the power, the energy of truth is well released, then everything becomes good and makes sense and there is no contrast to be made between solitude and community or anything else because everything is good.

It seems to me, though, that these streams do not get to run for me in the community and that I simply go along in the heavy, secure, confused neutrality of the community, though perhaps for others the springs are running. Then, instead of everything being one, everything (for me) merely gets confused. Though now, as a result of solitude, the Psalms in choir and especially the hymns and antiphons of Advent have all their old juice and much more too: a whole new mystery.

*　　*　　*

Guerric's beautiful fourth Advent sermon speaks of a grace and consecration given to the desert by Christ as he prayed in it. In the wilderness, Jesus prepared a new place for the new life and overcame evil by fasting not for himself "but for those who were to be the future dwellers in the wilderness." The desert is given us to get *the* evil, not just evil but the evil *one*, unnested from the crannies of our own hearts. Perhaps, again, my tendency to find this in solitude rather than community is simply subjective. After twenty-three years of communal routine, all the nests are well established. But in solitude and open air they are revealed and the wind blows on them and I know they must go.

December 8

A constant thumping and pummeling of guns at Fort Knox. It began last night when I was going to bed. Then there were big whumps, unlike cannons, more like some kind of missile. Now it sounds like a new kind of rapid-fire artillery, not the old rolling kind of the last war.

Undoubtedly, there are many who are willing to go to war in Asia or the Congo and once again repeat the madness of Vietnam and bring American power where the withdrawal of European colonialism seems to have left confusion and vacuum. Perhaps it seems that way to us because we are eager to have it that way. We *make* things be the way we need them to be.

The horrible Mississippi story (recent arrest of the sheriffs, etc., who are thought to have murdered the civil-rights workers last June), the obsession of Vietnam, the madness of patriots, all make this land seem possessed by a demonic illusion, driven to ruinous adventures by technological pride.

2:15. Bumps and punches at Fort Knox, faster and faster.

December 9

Last night I made a prayer vigil in the novitiate chapel, and I did not do a good job; I was somewhat disorganized and distracted. I went to bed late at the hermitage. All quiet. No lights at Boone's or Newton's. Cold. Lay in bed realizing what I was: I was *happy*!

I said the strange word, "happiness," and realized that it was there not as an "it" or object, it simply *was* and I was that.

And this morning, seeing the multitude of stars above the pine branches of the wood, I was suddenly hit, as it were, with the whole package of meaning of everything, that the immense mercy of God was upon me, that the Lord in infinite kindness had looked down on me, had given me this vocation out of love, and that He had always intended this. I saw how foolish and trivial had been all my fears and twistings and desperation! No matter what anyone else might do or say about it, however they might judge or evaluate it, all is irrelevant to the reality of my vocation to solitude even though I am not a typical hermit. Quite the contrary, perhaps.

It does not matter how I may or may not be classified, in the light of this simple fact of God's love and the form it has taken in the mystery of my life. Classifications are ludicrous and I have no further need to occupy my mind with them, at least not in this connection.

The only response is to go out from one's self with all that one is (which is nothing), and pour out that nothingness in gratitude that He is who He is.

All speech is impertinent. It destroys the simplicity of that nothingness before God by making it seem as if it had been something, as if it had something to say.

Who is like unto God?

December 10

Sister Luke came over from Loretto to talk to a dozen of us about the Council. She was the American woman auditor there this last session, one of the first group of such observers. Talking to her made the session very understandable, even the last couple of days, which were pretty ferocious. The great question is, what was Pope Paul trying to do? Was he supporting the conservatives against the liberals? Is he proving himself a "transition Pope" (whatever that means)? My guess is that he was simply trying, by means of curial politics, to keep things together as far as possible. But it also seems to me that he was much more acquiescent to the conservatives and their desires than to the liberals.

December 11

Sister Luke said that Archbishop Roberts, S.J., was not even allowed to give his intervention in the Council on conscientious objection. Can this be true? Perhaps only that he was one of several whose interventions on nuclear war had to be submitted in writing, or maybe not even that. But I note that Bishop Hannan's intervention, the official Pentagon line, was not only permitted but received much publicity in the American press. His speech and the similar hawk-like speech of the Bishop of Liverpool were among the few *reported in full* by the NCWC.

*   *   *

There was heavy rain all night. Now the rain on the roof accentuates the silence and surrounds the dryness and light of the hermitage as though with love and peace. The liberty and tranquillity of this place are indescribable, more than any bodily peace. This is a gift of God marked with His simplicity and His purity. How one's heart opens and what hope arises in the core of my being! It is as if I had not really hoped in God for years, as if I had been living all this time in despair.

Now all things seem reasonable and possible. A greater self-denial seems obvious and easy, though perhaps it may not turn out to be so. A whole new dimension of life is no longer a desperate dream but completely and simply credible.

December 16

Yesterday for the first time I was able to live a complete day's schedule as it ought to be, at least in this transition period at the hermitage. I came down only for my own Mass and dinner. I cooked supper at the hermitage and so forth. In fact, I cooked too much rice, having miscalculated, and sat half an hour consuming it with tea. But it was a splendid supper and I looked out at the hills in the clear evening light.

After that I washed the dishes: the bowl, the pot, the cup, the knife, the spoon. I looked up and saw a jet like a small rapid jewel, traveling north between the moon and the evening star, the moon being nearly full.

Then I went for a little walk, and looked out over the valley. Incredibly beautiful and peaceful. Blue hills, blue sky, woods, empty fields, lights going on in the abbey to the right through the screen of trees, hidden from the hermitage. And out there, lights in the three farms that I can see. One at Newton's and two others out there in the hills between here and New Hope.

Everything the Fathers of the Church say about the solitary life is exactly true. The temptations and the joys, above all, the tears and the ineffable peace and *happiness*. The happiness that is so pure because it is simply not one's own making but sheer mercy and gift. Happiness in the sense of having arrived at last in the place destined for me by God; of fulfilling the purpose for which I was brought here twenty-three years ago.

December 20, Fourth Sunday of Advent

I had permission to go and see Victor Hammer in Lexington Wednesday. He was thin and drawn, marked by sickness. He is unable to go out but works on his painting of the Resurrection. It was a pleasure to be in the beautiful little house on Market Street and to talk with him and Carolyn. Some very special Pedro Domecq brandy came out for the occasion, with excellent espresso coffee.

*   *   *

Two nights ago it turned very cold.

Yesterday morning, as I came down to the monastery in the bright frozen moonlight with the hard diamonded leaves crackling under my feet, a deer sprang up in the deep bushes of the hollow, perhaps two. I could see at least one in the moonlight.

*   *   *

I have finished an article for *Holiday*, "Rain and the Rhinoceros," and sent it yesterday.

*   *   *

Apparently the REA men have been around, as I can see stakes for poles, but just where I don't want them.

December 22

Lax sent me from Greece a typewritten copy of the trial in Leningrad of the poet Joseph Brodsky ("militant work-shy ebullient Brodsky"). It is as funny as a scene from Ionesco. Brodsky "belongs to a group where the word 'work' is greeted with satanic laughter" . . . "Brodsky has been defended by some coarse rascals, work-shy elements, loud-mouths and Beatles." In his diary, Brodsky had called Marx "an old glutton framed by a wreath of pine cones."

The only thing is, who is laughing? This was published in *Encounter*, and of course, *Time* picked it up. In what significant way does the mentality of *Time* readers differ from that of the people who condemned Brodsky? They are perhaps a little less crude, but are they any less square? Do they have any better ideas about poets and poetry or the value of work (the value of work measured by the money one makes and the status one gets, not by the work one does)?

(Fortunately, I am a success, I have status, I am in the *International Who's Who*, so I can be a hermit. Let others try!)

Anyway, I read the Brodsky trial on thin blue paper while eating breakfast in the hermitage. Yes, funny! But those idiots have the power to put him in a labor camp and keep him there.

*   *   *

The Epiphany antiphons are already running through my head. Also at chant practice yesterday, I realized how much I had grown to love the antiphons of Christmas Eve and Christmas Vespers.

I am finally reading Vladimir Lossky's fine book in French, *The Vision of God*, which reminds me that the best thing that has come out of the Council so far is the declaration on ecumenism: particularly the part on Oriental theology.

If it were a matter of choosing between contemplation and eschatology, there is no question that I am and would always be committed entirely to the latter. Here in the hermitage, returning necessarily to the beginnings, I know where my beginning was: hearing the name of God and of Christ preached in Corpus Christi Church in New York. I heard and I believed. And I believe that He has called me freely, out of pure mercy, to His love and salvation. That at the end, to which all is directed by His will, I shall see Him after I have put off my body in death and have risen together with Him to take up my body again. That at that Last Day all flesh shall see the salvation of God.

What this means is that my faith is an eschatological faith, not merely a means of penetrating the mystery of the Divine Presence, and dwelling in Him or serving Him here and now. Yet, because my faith is eschatological, it is also contemplative, for I am even here and now in the established kingdom. I can even now "see" something of the glory of that kingdom and praise Him who is King. I would be foolish then if I lived blindly, putting all seeing off until some imagined fulfillment, for my present seeing is the beginning of a real and unimaginable fulfillment.

Thus, contemplation and eschatology are one in Christian faith and in surrender to Christ. They complete each other and intensify each other. It is by contemplation and love that I can best prepare myself for the eschatological vision and best help the whole Church and all men to journey toward it.

The union of contemplation and eschatology is clear in the gift of the Holy Spirit. In Him we are awakened to know the Father because in Him we are refashioned in the likeness of the Son. And it is in this likeness that the Spirit will bring us at last to the clear vision of the invisible Father in the Son's glory, which will also be our glory.

Meanwhile, it is the Spirit who awakens in our hearts the faith and hope in which we cry for this eschatological fulfillment and vision. And in this hope there is already a beginning, a promise, a pledge, *"arrha,"* of the fulfillment. This is our contemplation: the realization and experience of the life-giving Spirit in whom the Father is present to us through the Son, our way, our truth and our light. The realization that we are on our way, that because we are on our way we are in the truth which is the end and by which we are already fully and eternally alive. Contemplation is the living sense of this life, this presence and this eternity. These words may mean nothing to many Catholics today. Maybe they have to be somehow translated. But they represent the faith I live by.

*   *   *

The guns were pounding at Fort Knox while I was making my afternoon meditation and I thought that, after all, this is no mere distraction. I am *here* because they are *there*; indeed, I am *supposed* to hear them! They form a part of an ever renewed decision and commitment, on my part, for peace. But what peace?

I am once again faced with the deepest ambiguities of political and social action. One thing is clear, that there is a will and intention of God bearing upon me, and I must let it bear fully on me, so that I may be free. My life has no meaning except as a conscious and total self-dedication to the *fulfillment of His intentions*, which, in their details, remain a complete mystery.

As far as I know it, I must seek to be a man wholly given to prayer here in this peace where I am, this silence in which He has put me. But I am far from being totally a man of prayer. Obviously, even writing is not excluded from a life of prayer. My will, however, cannot simply lose itself in this or that, in meditation or writing or study or tranquillity or work, but simply must surrender in all this, to the mysterious and sovereign intention of the Lord, the Master whom I have come here to serve.

I am not here to be this or that but to obey Him in everything —in *Gleichheit* (Eckhart)—and to learn slowly, patiently, the tempo of such obedience. If I had been a better cenobite, I would perhaps be more familiar with this obedience.

*   *   *

The REA men were here this morning. (Cold and misty.) The hermitage will tie into a line that will eventually go into a sewage-disposal plant to be built in the bottom by the creek. *O Beata Solitudo!*

December 23

For Eusebius, the Roman Empire had resolved the problem of conflicting nations, and conflicting angels of nations, against the one Lord. The angels and nations were subdued in one empire where the religion of the true God had taken over. Hence, the Pax Romana was, in effect, the peace in the Messianic kingdom. Hence, the emperor represented Christ on earth, the Prince of Peace, etc. We are still stuck with this dreadful ideology which set the power (angel) of the Roman Empire at the right hand of God.

For Origen, a man's "adversary" is his bad angel, deputed to keep him firmly in subjection *to the angelic power of his nation or of his tribe*, to see that he will not free himself. Our bad angel makes us love the nation above all instead of belonging only to God, in Christ, who is above all separate nations and has vanquished all the powers.

*   *   *

Danielou has said: "Material civilization in its demiurgic character seems to be one of the places where demonic action is most intense. Judeo-Christian tradition maintains the positive significance of political and cultural values. In this, it is opposed to the Gnostic doctrine of the *cosmocratores* but it recognizes that, in fact, these domains are invaded and dominated by demonic powers."

December 25

First Christmas at the hermitage. Very peaceful. No trouble sleeping, though there was, of all things, a thunderstorm. For two days the weather had been damp, windy and warm as it sometimes is in spring, and at one moment I even heard the frogs singing Christmas Eve!

The day before that, the novices were cutting down poplars and cedars in the field where the REA line needs to go through, and I finished some digging I thought I had to do to keep water from accumulating next to the cottage.

Before going down to the Midnight Mass, I got up and said vigils in the hermitage. All that is said in the Office about night, silence, shepherds and so forth sounds much better up here.

After that, I went down for Mass. The novices were happy around the Christmas tree and I was happy with them. The Midnight Mass was simpler than it has ever been.

*   *   *

St. Maximus says that he who "has sanctified his senses by looking with purity on all things" becomes like God. This is, I think, what the Zen Masters tried to do.

A letter from John Wu spoke of meeting Suzuki at Honolulu last summer. They talked of my meeting with Suzuki in New York. Suzuki said that he had intended to ask me a question but did not. "If God created the world, who created this Creator?" A good koan. The answer is *not* that of Augustine to the Arians, in the Lesson.

December 29, St. Thomas of Canterbury

On Christmas Day in the afternoon, Brother Colman and I drove over into the hills behind New Hope in the area where Edelin is giving the monastery some land for hermitages. As there is no road near the west end of that land, or I think not, we got some idea of it from the next valley, where the old ridge road goes from New Hope to Howardstown. Then we explored other such valleys, following the back roads as far as they went. The hills that look like a solid mass from the monastery are, of course, a labyrinth of deep silent wooded hollows with farms in the bottom. A whole world of wonderful hidden places, some very lost and wild. I am planning to get over there someday and spend the day on foot exploring the area around Edelin's and seeing where his land goes, if I can get any idea of the boundaries.

*   *   *

There was a little sun Christmas afternoon but the rest of the time has been gray and dark. I can't even remember what I did St. Stephen's afternoon when it was raining.

Yesterday, feast of the Holy Innocents. Brother Joachim was looking the hermitage over to plan the wiring for lights and for an electric stove to cook on.

*   *   *

I finished Von Durkheim on the "Japanese cult of tranquillity." The best and most revealing part is the appendix from a Japanese master of swordsmanship speaking of "the sword that kills and gives life" in the tradition of Takuin. Actually, the pinnacle of Japanese Zen swordsmanship is not violence and killing but simply a "truth" against which the opponent can ruin himself or by which he can be enlightened. A fascinating concept. Only what Paul would call "the animal man" needs to win ("prevail") but the spiritual man is simply true: and the law of truth has to win in him, because he lets it.

*　　*　　*

"Love comes from prayer and prayer from remaining in seclusion" (Isaac of Syria).

*　　*　　*

Certainly the break in my more solitary routine, going down to the monastery earlier without the long meditation, spending most of the day there, ceremonies, letters, and so forth, has created a kind of confusion, disturbance and laxity. This was made necessary by the feast days. But in the trouble itself and in the confusion I had to struggle for deeper conviction and commitment.

Solitude is not something to play with from time to time. It is going to be difficult to remain divided next year between hermitage and community; two tempos and two ways of life.

And yet, of course, I still need a good part of common life and will always need to maintain some definite contacts with the monastery. But it is hard and confusing to be uprooted from peace every time you begin barely to get into it; or rather not to be able to sink completely into unity and simplicity.

There is, of course, peace too in the community but it has a different and much more active rhythm.

However, in solitude, there must be, together with the fiery substance of the eternal prophets, also the terse anger and irony and humor of the Latin American poets with whom I am united in bonds of warmth and empathy, for instance the Peruvian Blanca Varela. I must translate her (a poem or two, sometime) and others—Jorge Eduard Eielson.

*   *   *

At last there is light again. First there were some stars here and there when I first got up at 2:15. Then a surprise. In an unexpected corner of the woods, the thin last slice of leftover moon, the last moon of 1964. The sun came up at 8:05. Our time here is unnatural, as we are on Eastern Standard.

Then there was the extraordinary purity and stillness and calm of that moment of sunrise and renewal. Peace of the woods and the valley. Out there somewhere a heifer salutes the morning with enthusiastic lowing.

1965

January 1

I woke up this morning with the vague feeling that something was walking around the hermitage. It was the rain again. So begins the imagined New Year. Yet it is too well imagined, and the date, 1965, on the new ordo confounds me. My Mass was fine and so was the Thanksgiving afterward. The last thing I read before going to bed in the old year was a letter of Peter Damian to hermits, recently republished by Dom Leclercq. They wanted to be buried, when they died, at their hermitage and nowhere else. I can well agree with that!

I got a fine letter from John Wu and a chapter of his new book (in progress), *The Golden Age of Zen*, a good chapter on Hui Neng. Also a letter from Webster College, where they will want the exhibit of drawings in April. A card from the Polish Marxist who was here with a group from Indiana University. When was it?

I had a long talk with Brother Basil McMurray, who thinks he will leave here when his simple vows run out, to go to Mount Savior, but on a special basis.

*   *   *

It seems to be a mistake to read in uninterrupted succession in the refectory one speech after another by Pope Paul, just as it was a mistake to try to read all the Council interventions. One becomes very oppressed with the jargon, the uniform tone of official optimism and inspirationalism and so forth. Yet the Pope did say a few good things both at Bombay and in his Christmas message on peace, emphasizing the need for disarmament, speaking against nationalism, the arms race, and the stockpiling of overkill weapons.

January 4

Even worse than Council speeches in the refectory was Archbishop O'Boyle's "explanation" of the last two agitated days of the Council. And then, after that, the *Time* story on the murder of hostages in Stanleyville, Congo, last November. A tragic thing. But the *Time* story, equally tragic, assumes fantastic perspectives. No indication that anybody could possibly be wrong except the African rebels, and that the Tshombe Belgian–American intervention is the only thing that could possibly be reasonable, human, etc. Were the hostages martyrs to a Red plot or also to the greed of the people who want to hold on to the mines in Katanga? The trouble is that indignation and horror swept the community (and they should) but with them also a complete conviction that of course the implied judgment and interpretation of *Time* were both satisfactory and final.

When you think that in all the country it is this way, about Cuba, Vietnam, the Congo, etc., what can possibly become of it but one dirty adventure and war on top of another?

Use of torture in Vietnam by our side is admitted, without apology, as something quite reasonable.

January 6

Yesterday was extraordinary. I had planned to take a whole day of recollection out in the hills around Edelin's hollow to explore the place and get some idea of where it goes and what is around it. Fortunately, Edelin came along with Brother Colman, who drove me out in the Scout, to show me where one could get into his property from the top of the hills on the west. It was wonderful wild country and I had a great day.

We left the monastery about 8:15, started back into the knobs to the southwest of New Hope and climbed the narrow country road that clings to the steep hillside above Old Coon Hollow, not to be confused, says Edelin, with Coon Hollow.

At the top of the rise we got into a rolling tableland of scrub oak and sassafras, with deep hollows biting into it. A very old road runs along the watershed between the Rolling Fork valley and the other valley where Edelin's house used to be. It is a magnificent wild, scrubby, lost road. The sun was bright and the air was not too cold.

I got off near where the woods slope down, about a mile, into Bell Hollow at the top, amid the thick tangle of trees and wild grapevines near a collapsed house. In a half-cleared area, there are still pear trees and Edelin says the deer like to come and eat the pears. Here too in a gully is a spring which feeds the stream running through Edelin's pasture. Actually, one of several streams that join there.

Edelin and Brother Colman left me there and I went down to the spring, found it without trouble. Wonderful clear water pouring strongly out of the cleft in the mossy rock. I drank from it in my cupped hands and suddenly realized it was years, perhaps twenty-five or thirty years, since I had tasted such water. Absolutely pure and clear and sweet with the freshness of untouched water. No chemicals.

I looked up at the clear sky and the tops of the leafless trees shining in the sun and it was a moment of angelic lucidity. I said the Psalms of Tierce with great joy, overflowing joy, as if the land and woods and spring were all praising God through me. Again the sense of angelic transparency of everything: of pure, simple and total light.

The word that comes closest to pointing to it is "simple." It was all so simple, but with a simplicity to which one seems to aspire, only seldom to attain it. A simplicity that is and has and says everything just because it is simple.

After that I scrambled around a bit on the steep rocky hillside in the sun to get oriented and then started through the thick sassafras out on a long wooded spur which I guessed would overlook Bell Hollow: and it did.

After about a half mile through very thick brush with vines and creepers and brambles and much young growth, bigger trees being damaged by fire, I came to the end. I could see the hollow in haze against the sun. I could see the point of the pasture on the hillside a mile or so away where the three walnut trees grow and, of course, the other side of the valley and the county road. Most of the view was of knobs and woods. A sea of sun and haze, silence and trees.

I sat there a long time, said Sext, read a letter from Milosz (an important letter too) and had a marvelous box lunch which Leone Gannon at the ladies' guesthouse got up for me. (She is Brother Colman's mother.) And as time went on I was more and more under the spell of the place until finally about twelve the sky began to cloud over.

The SAC planes. I forgot to mention that when I was at the spring after Tierce, when I was about to leave, the huge SAC plane announced its coming and immediately swooped exactly overhead, not more than two or three hundred feet above the hilltops. It was fantastic and sure enough I could see the trap door of the bomb bays. The whole thing was an awesome part of the "simplicity," a sign and an "of course." It had a great deal to do with all the rest of the day.

During the day, in fact, five SAC planes went over all on the same course, swooping over the hills. Not all exactly over this particular hollow but all visible from it, i.e., very close, within a mile. Otherwise, one could not see them flying so low with so many hills around. Only the first and the last went directly over me, but directly so that I was looking right up at the bomb. This was quite fantastic. Of course, the mere concept of fear was utterly meaningless, out of the question. I felt only an intellectual and moral intuition, a sort of "of course," which seemed to be part of the whole day and of its experience.

*   *   *

Near the collapsed house on the ridge is a clearing with rubbish lying around, beer cans with bullet holes in them, a pair of shoes, chewing-gum wrappers, etc. It used to be, said Edelin, a "dance hall," a place where people from the hollows came up to get drunk and raise hell. It is near the spring but far from the hollow. Of this particular area, incidentally, Freddie Hicks, who lives on the other side of the road down by New Hope, says: "When you get beyond this road, you leave civilization!"

*   *   *

I went down a logging trail. Many trees were cut this fall and winter. A beautiful wet trail into the hollow, full of tall beech trees and other hardwoods. Most of the mature oaks had just been cut.

A lovely silent walk with streams full of clear water and I suddenly came out into Edelin's pasture in Bell Hollow at the bottom. The place just took my breath away. I had seen it before in September but without this angelic light. Now the sun was hidden and the sky overcast but there was a sense of blessed silence and joy. And once again that perfect simplicity.

I wandered up and down the hollow in the empty pasture, tasting the void, silence and peace, went up the hillside where the two knob hawks came out screaming and wheeled over to the other side of the valley. I found the old half-burnt barn, belonging to one of Edelin's neighbors in a branch of the hollow. I began the Office of Epiphany in the open space where there are still stones from the foundations of the slaves' house. I could use them as foundations for a house of my own.

I went back to my place, sat on a felled white oak and looked down at the hollow until I had to go. The last SAC plane went over again, right overhead, and the bomb pointed to the chosen place. I read a blessing over the valley from the breviary. Never has a written prayer meant so much. I know one day there will be hermits here, or men living alone, but I think the hollow is already blessed because of the slaves that were there. Perhaps one or other of them was very holy.

*   *   *

So I went back up the logging trail and met Brother Colman and Edelin in the Scout on the ridge, coming along the old road. Never was there such a day.

January 8
When I got back and calmed down the other evening, I realized that I was being very enthusiastic and unreasonable. All day Epiph-

any I had a sort of emotional hangover from that day out in Bell Hollow. I sat at the top of the field next to the hermitage looking down at the cottage and I tried to meditate sanely in the sun. I came out of it much quieter and cooked myself some supper, a thin potato soup made out of dust from an envelope.

Then, as the sun was setting, I looked up at the end of the field where I had sat in the afternoon and suddenly realized that there were beings there—deer. In the evening light they were hard to descry against the tall brown grass, but I could pick out at least five.

They stood still looking at me and I stood looking at them. A lovely moment that stretched into ten minutes or more. They did not run, though kids could be heard shouting somewhere down by the waterworks, but eventually they walked quietly away into the tall grass and bushes and, for all I know, they slept there. When they walked they seemed to multiply, so that in the end I thought there must be at least ten of them.

*   *   *

As for the SAC plane, it is perfectly impartial. Yesterday afternoon, as I was saying Office on the walk below the novitiate before going to see the abbot, the planes swooped by right over my hermitage. I would say it was hardly one hundred and fifty feet above the treetops.

*   *   *

I spoke to Father Abbot about Bell Hollow and he said there could be no question of anybody going there until the monastery had title to the land. He is also thinking of buying other property next to Edelin's so that the place will be protected. He seems quite intent on eventually having hermitages there. It is clearly not yet time to be thinking of moving there myself, and I am very doubtful whether I should really think of that at all. I have this place now and I have just begun to really live in it. Brother Joachim is slowly getting it wired up for electric light, etc., and there is an old beat-up electric stove to cook my soup on when it has current to work with.

January 9

Again last night in the warm dark, before the plentiful rain, a plane again—though perhaps smaller than the big SAC—came right over the hermitage in the dark, a cross of four lights, a technological swan.

> *La espesa rueda de la tierra*
> *Su llanto húmedo de olvido*
> *Hace rodar, cortando el tiempo*
> *En mitades inaccesibles.*   (Neruda)

> *Its wet complaint of forgetting*
> *Is what makes turn the world's thick wheel,*
> *Cutting time*
> *Into inaccessible halves.*

*   *   *

I am full of rice which I found a new good way of cooking. Peace, silence.

January 10

Jaspers says (and this is analogous to a basic principle and J. Ellul also): "Once I envision world history or life's entirety as a kind of finite totality, I can act only on the basis of sham knowledge, in distortion of actual possibilities, far from reality, vague about facts, achieving nothing but confusion and advancing in directions altogether different from those I wanted" (*Nietzsche and Christianity*). This applies also to monastic reform.

Jaspers again: "Whenever my knowledge is chained to total concepts, whenever my actions are based on a specific world view, I am distracted from what I am really able to do. I am cheated of the present for the sake of something imagined, past or future, rather than real which has not been actually lived and has never been realized."

(Note that in "monastic ideals," this is precisely the problem. One assumes that the ideal was once fully real and actually lived in a golden age and, thus, one claims to have every reason for resentment at the unrealization of what cannot be and *never was* real. In actual fact, the true monks had a reality which was quite different and fitted in entirely and precisely with their own special and fully accepted circumstances.)

Another quote from Jaspers: "The man who keeps faith with reality wants to act truthfully in the here and now, not to derive a secondhand here and now from a purpose."

There is a problem of false, so-called Christian historicism which sets up history as a unity that "can be comprehended." Nietzsche did and did not see this danger. He may have fallen into it himself, but he said that *because of this* change of focus centered on history, "God was dead" and his death was the fault of Christianity.

Nietzsche also made his classic analysis of Christian morality and the Christian will to truth being, in the end, self-destructive. The ultimate end of Christian will to truth was to destroy even itself by doubts, said Nietzsche. (Thus, Christianity ends in nihilism.)

We certainly see something of this in monasticism today. With the breakdown of confidence in authority and the insatiable thirst for an "authentic ideal," monks are becoming incapable of accepting and resting in anything. Yet they do not really seek God, they seek a perfect monasticism.

All that Nietzsche said about Christianity immediately becomes true as soon as one puts anything else before God, whether it be history or culture or science or contemplation or liturgy or reform or justice. But Jaspers has a brilliant insight into the real possibilities of Nietzsche. If all is permitted, then there is an alternative to the nihilism of despair: the nihilism of strength, "drawn from the vastness of the encompassing and able to do without ties to supposedly finite objectives, maxims and laws." Is not this Christianity?

"It needs no such ties because from the depths of the encompassing, it will always come upon what is true and what is to be done. It will know historically and with the tranquillity of eternity."

Maybe. But it seems to me that the Gospel says this and the Gospel remains necessary if men are to attain this freedom rightly, not fall into the fanaticism and arbitrariness which are rooted in despair.

In any case, Jaspers certainly shows the difference between the popular residue of Nietzsche's anti-Christianity and its really profound implication. He ends with Nietzsche's curse on his own admirers: "To this mankind of today, I will not be light nor be called light! Those I will blind!"

*　　*　　*

Thank God that after NCWC reports of this or that speech of the Pope in the refectory, we are finally getting back to Meriol Trevor's biography of Newman. I have missed it for three months. It is a very good book.

January 11

I spoke too soon. The NCWC reports started all over again yesterday, Sunday.

*　　*　　*

A little Nietzsche is stimulating, no doubt, but what I really like to read is Isaac of Nineveh in the hermitage or Zen Masters in the fields.

I like to say Lauds of the Little Office of the Blessed Virgin by heart when I am coming down through the woods by starlight with everything there, stars and light, frost and cold, ice and snow, trees, earth, hills and, cozy in the lighted monastery, the sons of men.

January 17

Brilliant night, deep snow sparkling in the moon. Difficult to get this ball-point pen to write, it is so cold; but a good fire keeps the front room of the hermitage fairly warm and I think it will be wonderful walking down to the monastery in an hour or so. The snow began in the early morning yesterday and by the time I started down to the monastery it was blowing in my eyes so that I had to keep them half closed. It blew and snowed all day.

In the monastery after dinner, I played to the novices Brother Antoninus' record *The Tongs of Jeopardy*. It is remarkably good. A meditation on the Kennedy assassination. Brother Antoninus was speaking about this when he was here and I was quite struck by his ideas at that time. They cannot be summed up as "Jungian" but he has remarkable and sensitive poetic insight into the state of the American mind—better than anything else I know. For instance, how much deeper than Paul Goodman's *Growing Up Absurd*, which I have just recently read. More than Jungian, the *Tongs* meditation is deeply Biblical; and his intuition of the Cain idea, the drive to fratricide as the great weakness in the American psyche, is most impressive and I think great.

Illtud Evans is coming here to preach the retreat and I will talk to him about this.

I am tempted to review Brother Antoninus' *Tongs of Jeopardy* for *Blackfriars*.

Showing how the Kennedy assassination moved people, rightly or wrongly, sanely or otherwise, one of our brothers did a drawing, nothing to do with the Antoninus record, of a crucifixion and on the cross was Jacqueline Kennedy (!!). A failure of taste and full of implication. A concept that to me is unintelligible. She, of course, was central in the whole thing. Brother Antoninus had little to say of her in *Tongs*. I wonder why. Perhaps the Irish keening at the end was meant to carry what could not be articulated about her and her grief.

My feeling was that the relationship to her, in which we all ended up, was the most significant thing of all, as if she had redeemed us from all the evil of the murder and of the national sin. (Of course, I suppose that was the idea of the brother who did the drawing.)

She stood out as a presence of love, nobility, truth and decision; as one who chose to be as she was and to forgive inexplicably and be loved and admired and yet to stand above all relationships and bear witness to a kind of deep truth in the whole thing which enabled the mind of the nation to get itself back together again, to collect itself again, relate itself once again to identity and truth.

In other words, it was she who did the greatest thing of all and the noblest thing: disinterestedly and without strings, deciding on her own with great courage and intuition to point to the truth and allow everybody else to see what she was pointing to and decide accordingly. Thanks to the TV presentation of it, I understand, very many people did come up with a noble and honest and contrite decision. But, on the other hand, many did not. Dallas remained "without sin."

Brother Antoninus contrasted the funeral rites of Kennedy with the mendacity of conventions and the lying quality of so much in American life. In any case, Jacqueline Kennedy gave America a sense of being *true* which we seldom get in public life.

When I step out on the porch the bristles in my nose instantly freeze up and the outdoor jakes is a grievous shock. The temperature must be zero or below.

Inside the house the thermometer by the door says forty-five but it is unreliable. I am warm close to the fire but have plenty of clothes on. The whole valley is bright with moonlight and snow and perfectly silent.

* * *

Last week I wrote the preface to Phil Berrigan's book *No More Strangers*, in which there are some fine ideas and some bad writing.

January 19

Very cold again. Snow still fairly deep but a bright day. Father Illtud Evans began our retreat last night. Sister Luke came over with him from Loretto yesterday. She is now on a subcommittee working on Schema 13 for the Council, one of the first women to be in such a position, and she wanted to talk about the work of the committee and the schema. I gave her what ideas I had, and I think that as long as they don't take account of the real problem posed by technology, anything they say or do will be beside the point.

January 21

I spent another good day in Bell Hollow. Snow, sun, peace. This was yesterday.

I explored a little more, climbed back up the gully to the spring and came down again by the logging trail. All was undisturbed snow except for the tracks of dogs and rabbits, though at the top of the ridge, on the old wagon road to Howardstown, were the steps of a man who had been there probably the day before. Father Abbot came out there with Brother Nicholas and I ran into him, which I did not particularly want to do. The talk got around to electric fences, boundary lines, snakes, etc. He is very interested in the place and, first of all, acquiring the place. He is full of ideas and deals. And Edelin is dealing with somebody whose name sounds like Cruise, getting ready to trade something for something else. The big trees have been cut off Cruise's land and the tops are lying around all over the place. Cruise, it is said, buys only in order to sell and so on. Cruise owns the valley where the ruined barn is and this is right next to Edelin's, so that, if we wanted to be fully protected, we would have to have it. Besides, his valley would be good for hermitages too. I saw it yesterday and it goes back deep into the hills.

But when I think of all this dealing and organizing and planning and so on and the institution that might finally result, the whole thing becomes much less interesting. Would I be a fool if I went along with all this? Perhaps I would. Would it not be much wiser and simpler to stay where I am and make the best of it for the moment? I am clearly on my own and I no longer have to make any more plans and I am arousing no comment in the community and I am, above all, dependent upon no one. My hermitage is a very decent and beautiful solitude which no longer arouses any comment, is not particularly criticized, gives nobody any trouble, enables me to take care of myself without relying on anybody else, it is close to the monastery, I can get what I need at any moment, nobody has to bring things to me, whereas, if I went to Bell Hollow, I would be completely dependent on others coming out there, unless they gave me a jeep: in which case there would be a great deal of running around. All this is something to think of.

January 22

Vintila Horia sent me his novel about Plato in French. Horia is a Romanian novelist. I find it extraordinarily beautiful, a sustained tone of wisdom with all kinds of modern undertones. Very actual.

Plato says in the novel: "I saw the world rushing into stupidity with such natural self-assurance that it caused me to suffer keenly, as if I had been personally responsible for it, while the people around me saw the future as a new pleasure to be expected from a certain joy: as if by being born into the world they acquired a right to this" (p. 101).

Meanwhile, an ex-novice, Bill Grimes, sent a copy of the *Kiplinger News Letter* which wound up 1964 with the gift of prophecy, peering into the glad future of 1980. Millions more people but no nuclear war, no world war but more, more, more of everything. More superhighways, more cities rebuilt, more suburbs, more money.

He ignores the question whether all these more people will have more jobs.

More recreation, more fun, more colleges and even, with all the money around, a boom in art, music and literature.

(I just can't wait to be sixty-five, still not fully able to believe I will make it to fifty in nine days' time.) Will I see this glorious future in which he does, nevertheless, hint at the possibility of problems?

What a total lack of imagination! The prophecy is unimaginative enough to be perhaps even *true*, but how intolerable. Nothing to look forward to but the same inanities, falsities, clichés, and pretenses. But there will surely be more frustration, therefore more madness, violence, degeneracy, addiction. The country will be one vast asylum.

I have higher hopes. I dare to hope for *change*, not only quantitative but qualitative too; such change must come through darkness and crisis, not joyous and painless adventure. Perhaps I say that out of habit.

January 25
Father Illtud has been preaching a good retreat. We took a couple of walks together and had some long conversations on gray windy afternoons. Talked about Cambridge and *Blackfriars* and the new colleges and the Hebrides. (On Rum now they allow no one to live except those protecting the wildlife and trying to restore the original ecology. This is wonderful.)

137

January 27

The retreat ended yesterday. Father Illtud tired with a cold. John Howard Griffin came to see Illtud and I saw John briefly. He spoke of a bombing in Youngstown, Ohio, the house of some Negroes who moved into a white neighborhood. Now it all moves North. He says my stuff on the race issue was by no means too pessimistic. Some reviewers are indignantly stating that it is.

*   *   *

There was a concelebrated Mass at the end of the retreat, the first one we have had here after some difficulties with the bishop, not just obstruction but meticulous observation. It was solemn and impressive and I think a very great grace for the community and a fine ending for the retreat. I was not one of the concelebrants, as I preferred to watch this time, and I also wanted to be sure not to exclude someone else who is more keen on the liturgy than I am. The number this time was limited. I am near the top of the list, so I might exclude one of the junior priests if I signed up for it. Actually, only three priests senior to me got in on it, Fathers Joseph, Raymond and Roger. But it was a great festival. A little overlong due to excessive slowness and delay, for instance, purifying patens, chalices, etc., at the end.

The Communion of the concelebrants went extremely slowly, still it was quite impressive.

After the Mass, I came out into a high wind and a strange mauve fog, a dust storm from somewhere. The infirmary refectory was full of dust at the dinner. A swinging window was smashed and fell in the elevator shaft, where there are still windows. The fire alarm went off and everything was in confusion. I was buried under the avalanche of mail they had obligingly saved up over the retreat.

Best thing in the mail, two books from Nicanor Parra. I would love to translate some of it. Maybe I will do a book of translations from Parra and Pessõa and call it "Two Anti-Poets." I think I will write Laughlin about this. But I will not neglect Chuang Tzu.

January 30

A cold night. I woke up to find the night completely filled with the depth and silence of snow. I stayed up here (at the hermitage) for supper last night, but having cooked soup, cut up a pear and a banana for dessert, and made toast, I finally came to the conclusion that it was all much too elaborate. If there were no better reason for fasting, the mere fact of saving time would be a good enough reason. The bowl and saucepan have to be washed and I have only a bucket of rainwater for washing them in, etc. Taking only coffee for breakfast makes a lot of sense because then I can read quietly and sip my mug of coffee at leisure and it really suffices for the morning.

*   *   *

There is a great need for discipline in meditation. Reading helps, the early-morning hours are good, though, in the morning meditation, I am easily distracted by the fire. An hour is not much, but I can be more meditative in the hours of reading which follow and which go much too fast. This can be two hours if I go down later to the monastery, which on Sundays I do. In the afternoon, work takes up so much time and there can be so much of it. Just keeping the place clean is already a big task. Then there is wood to be chopped, etc. The fire is voracious but it is pleasant company.

Today I sent off to *Holiday* a revised version of "Rain and the Rhinoceros" (which is also being censored).

A telegram came yesterday from New Orleans that my drawings had not arrived there.

*   *   *

The vigil of my fiftieth birthday. A bright snowy afternoon. Delicate blue clouds of snow blowing down off the frozen trees. I forcibly restrained myself from much work around the hermitage, made sure of my hour's meditation and will do more later. How badly I need it. I realize how great is the tempo and pressure of work I have been in down at the community, with too many irons in the fire.

True, I have there gained the knack of dropping everything, completely relaxing my attention and forgetting the work by going out and looking at the hills. And the novitiate work is not exceedingly absorbing. My biggest trouble now is letter writing.

*   *   *

Shall I look at the past as if it were something to analyze and think about? Rather, I thank God for the present, not for myself in the present but for the present which is His and in Him. As for the past, I am inarticulate about it now. I can remember irrelevant moments of embarrassment here and there and my joys seemed to have been, to a great extent, meaningless. Yet, as I sit here in this wintry, lonely, quiet place, I suppose I am the same person as the eighteen-year-old riding alone back into Bournemouth in a bus out of the New Forest, where I had camped a couple of days and nights alone. I suppose I regret most my lack of love, my selfishness, my glibness, which covered a profound shyness and an urgent need for love. My glibness with girls who after all did love me, I think, for a time. My fault was my inability to believe it and my efforts to get complete assurance and perfect fulfillment.

I suppose I am still the person that lived for a while at 71 Bridge Street, Cambridge, and had Sabberton for my tailor. He made me that strange Alphonse Daudet coat and the tails I wore perhaps twice. Once to the Boat-race Ball, where I was very selfish and unkind to Joan. And Clare was my college and I was a damned fool, sitting on the steps of the boathouse late at night with Sylvia . . . things like that. Adventures.

What I find most in my whole life is illusion, wanting to be something of which I have formed a concept. I hope I will get free of all that now, because that is going to be the struggle and yet I have to be something that I ought to be. I have to meet a certain demand for order and inner light and tranquillity, God's demand, that is, that I remove obstacles to His giving me all these.

Snow, silence, the talking fire, the watch on the table, sorrow. What would be the use of going over all this? I will just get cleaned up (my hands are dirty) and say the Psalms of my birthday:

> Yet you drew me out of the womb
> you entrusted me to my mother's breasts
> placed on your lap from my birth
> from my mother's womb you have been my God.

(Ps. 21 [22])

No matter what mistakes and delusions have marked my life, most of it I think has been happiness and, as far as I can tell, truth. There were whole seasons of insecurity, largely when I was under twenty-one and followed friends who were not really my own kind. But in my senior year at Columbia things got straight.

I can remember many happy and illumined days and whole blocks of time that were fruitful. There were a few nightmare times in my childhood, but at Saint-Antonin life was a real revelation. Then again at so many various times and places. In Sussex, at Rye, in the country, at Olean to spend Christmas with Lax. Arrivals and departures on the Erie were generally great. The cottage on the hill too. Then Cuba, wonderful days there. All this I have said before and the whole world knows it.

Here? The profoundest and happiest times of my life have been in and around Gethsemani, but also some of the most terrible. Mostly, the happy moments were in the woods and fields along with the sky and the sun and up here at the hermitage and with the novices afternoons at work. Good moments, too, with Protestants coming here, especially the Hammers and, of course, on one or two visits to Lexington.

Good visits with J. Laughlin, Ping Ferry, good days in Louisville with Jim Wygal; but the deepest happiness has always been when I was alone, either here in the hermitage or in the novice master's room (that wonderful summer of the gardenias and Plato), or simply out in the fields.

Of course, there was the old vault too, and I must mention many happy moments with the students when I was their Father Master. Also a couple of good days in the hospital when I was well enough to go out and walk around near the grotto.

I could fill another page just with names of people I have loved to be with and loved to hear from. Lax, above all, and Mark Van Doren and all the old friends, Ad Reinhardt and so on. Naomi and Bob Giroux, and all my Latin American friends—Ernesto Cardenal and Pablo Antonio Cuadra. So many students and novices especially, for some reason, the group that came in 1960 and 1961. Brothers Cuthbert, Dennis, Basil and so forth; so many others that have left, like Father John of the Cross. Why go on? Thank God for all of them.

January 31

I can imagine no greater cause for gratitude on my fiftieth birthday than that, on it, I woke up in a hermitage. Fierce cold all night, certainly down to zero, but I have no outdoor thermometer.

Inside the house, it almost froze, though embers still glowed under the ashes in the fireplace. The cold woke me up at one point, but I adjusted the blankets and went back to sleep. What more do I seek than this silence, this simplicity, this "living together with wisdom"? For me, there is nothing else, and to think that I have had the grace to taste a little of what all men really seek without realizing it! All the more obligation to have compassion and love, and to pray for them.

*   *   *

Last night before going to bed I realized momentarily what solitude really means. When the ropes are cast off and the ship is no longer tied to land but heads out to sea without ties and without restraint, not the sea of passion, but the sea of purity and love that is without care. The vastness that loves God alone immediately and directly in Himself as the All, and the seeming nothing that is all. The unutterable confusion of those who think that God is a mental object and that to "love God alone" is to exclude all other objects and concentrate on this one! Fatal. Yet that is why so many misunderstand the meaning of contemplation and solitude and condemn it.

But I see too that I no longer have the slightest need to argue with these people. I have nothing to justify, nothing to defend. I need only defend this vast simple emptiness from my own self and the rest is clear.

*   *   *

The beautiful jeweled shining of honey in the lamplight. Festival!

*   *   *

A thought that came to me during meditation: The error of racism is the logical consequence of an essentialist style of thought. Finding out what a man is and then nailing him down to his definition so that he can never change. A white man is a white man and that is it. A Negro, even though he be three parts white, is a Negro with all that our rigid definition predicates of a Negro. And so the logical machine can grind him down and devour him because of his essence.

Do you think that, in an era of existentialism, this will get any better? On the contrary, definitions, more and more schematic, are fed into computers. The machines are meditating on the most arbitrary and rudimentary of essences punched into IBM cards and defining you and me forever without appeal. "A priest, a Negro, a Jew, a socialist." (Problem of the Mexican intellectual and editor García Torres and his passport trouble because some idiot in an embassy punched his card as "Red.")

February 2
Again it is very cold. On the 31st, it went down to about four below. This morning it is about zero. Yesterday it was warmer. It went up all the way to twenty-eight and there was more snow.

A great deal of wood I have for the fire is wet or not sufficiently seasoned to burn well, though finally, this morning, I got a pretty hot fire going with a big cedar log on top of it. This is some of the coldest weather we have had in the twenty-three years I have been here, but sleeping was fine, certainly no worse than anywhere else. In fact, I was very snug under a big pile of blankets.

*　　*　　*

It is hard but good to live according to nature, with a primitive technology of wood-chopping and fires, rather than according to the mature technology which has supplanted nature, creating its own weather. Yet there are advantages too in a warmed house and a self-stoking furnace. There is no need to pledge allegiance to either of these systems. Just get warm in any way you can and love God and pray.

*　　*　　*

I see more and more that now I must desire nothing else than to be "poured out as a libation" to give and surrender my being without concern. The cold woods make this more real; and so does the loneliness.

Coming up last night at the time of a very cold sunset, I found two little birds still picking at crumbs I had left for them on the frozen porch. Everywhere else, snow.

In the morning, coming down, all the tracks covered by snow blown over the path by the wind except tracks of the cat that hunts around the old sheep barn.

Solitude; being aware that you are one man in this snow where there has been no one else but one cat.

February 4

The cold weather finally let up a bit today, the first time in about a week that it has been above freezing. Zero nights or ten above, very cold, sometimes even in bed.

I had the night watch in the monastery last night and came back through the frozen woods to a very cold cottage. But today the snow melted in part and ran loquaciously from the gutters of my roof into buckets. Water again for dishwashing. The bucket I had collected last time was nearly finished.

In my fireplace, I am burning shelves from the old monastic library: not the chestnut shelves, but the sides of poplar. They are dry and quickly make a good hot blaze.

*   *   *

The new library was formally opened in the former brothers' novitiate building on Sunday, my birthday. I was very happy with it. The stacks are well lighted, a big pleasant room with desks was formerly a dormitory, and the reading room upstairs is pleasant too. It is too far for me to go often, but I am glad of the change.

*   *   *

Last night I had a curious and moving dream about a "black mother." I was in a place somewhere I had been as a child. I could not recognize it, but also there seemed to be some connection with Bell Hollow and I realized that I had come there for a reunion with a Negro foster mother whom I had loved in my childhood in the dream. Indeed it seemed, in the dream, that I owed my life to her, to her love for me, so that it was really she and not my natural mother who had given me life, as if from her had come a new life.

And there she was. Her face was ugly and severe, yet a great warmth came from her to me and we embraced with love. I felt deep gratitude, and what I recognized was not her face but the warmth of her embrace and of her heart, so to speak. Then we danced a little together, I and my black mother.

Finally I had to continue the journey that I was on in my dream. I cannot remember any more about this journey or any incidents connected with it. The comings and goings, the turning back and so forth.

*　　*　　*

Today, besides a good letter from Gordon Zahn and other pleasant things in the mail, came a fantastic present from Daisetz Suzuki. A scroll with some of his calligraphies superbly done. The scroll in a perfect little box, the whole thing utterly splendid. I never saw anything so excellent. It will be wonderful in the hermitage, but I have no clue to what the characters say.

Also there was a letter from John Pick saying he wanted my drawings for exhibit for Marquette in Milwaukee. They are now at Xavier University in New Orleans.

February 9

I must admit that I am still very much moved by Horace, as, for instance, a quote from the Second Epode which I ran across by chance when leafing through the *Liber Confortatorius* of Goscelin in the eleventh-century letter to a recluse. The structure and clarity and music of Horace are great. He is *not* trite (I used to think he was!). There is, it seems to me, real depth there and this is shown by the sustained purity and strength of his tone. Something quite untranslatable.

*　　*　　*

Rereading the issue of *La Vie Spirituelle* on solitude in 1952, I am struck by the evident progress that has been made. In those days, the tone was not one of real hope, simply a statement of the deplorable fact that the hermit life had practically ceased to exist and that religious superiors could not be brought to see its meaning and importance. Now, on the contrary, it is once again a fact and we are moving beyond the stage where it was thought necessary for a monk to get exclaustrated in order to be a solitary. In other words, beyond the time when it was necessary for a monk to leave the monastic order in order to fulfill his monastic vocation. I am working on a paper about this for a meeting of canonists (to which I will certainly not be going) at New Melleray this spring.

February 11

There has been depressing news from Vietnam. Because of the successful guerrilla attacks of the Vietcong on American bases in South Vietnam, there has been bombing of towns and bases in North Vietnam and signs today are going around the monastery that there was a big bombing evidently of a city by our planes. Perhaps Hanoi has been bombed.

All I can feel is disgust and hopelessness. Have people no understanding left and not even a memory? Haven't they enough imagination to see how totally useless and absurd the whole thing is, even if they lack the moral sense to see the injustice of it? The whole effect of this will be to make America more hated, just as the Russians were hated after the Hungarian revolt in 1956. There is no better way than this to promote Communism in Asia. We are driving people to it instead of "liberating" them from it.

*   *   *

Today I finished the first draft of my paper on eremitism.

*   *   *

Rain all day. I did not get back to the hermitage until after supper. It seems that everything looks favorable for my moving up here when Father Callistus gets back from Rome. But now there is doubt about Father Flavian taking the novice master's job because he wants to go to the Camaldolese, of all things, which sounds foolish to me.

*   *   *

Nightfall. Wind from the west. The porch shines with rain and low dark rags of clouds blow over the valley. The rain becomes more furious and the air is filled with voices and with what might sound like confused radio music in another building—but there is no other building. The sound seems to be coming to a brassy crescendo and ending, but it does not end.

Also the jet planes. High in the storm are jet planes.

Today I got the censor's approval for "Rain and the Rhinoceros," written in December. But the rain is different this time, more serious, less peaceful, more talkative. A very great deal of talk.

February 14

The other day a letter came from Godfrey Diekmann asking me to participate in an ecumenical meeting at Collegeville together with Father Häring, Dom Leclercq, Father Barnabas Ahern and, on the other side, Douglas Steere and nine others. I asked Father Abbot and this permission, which in the circumstances I think any other superior would have granted, was refused.

It is not that I had my heart set on going, about that I can be indifferent. I would have liked to go because I think, for one thing, it would have done me good and I would have learned a lot. I would have had the grace of having done something for the Church and of having participated in a dialogue that would be evidently blessed and fruitful.

It was not possible to discuss anything about this with the abbot. In fact, there was no discussion of why I should *not* go. No real reasons were given, just emotion on the part of the abbot.

He got that look compounded of suffering and stubbornness, interpretable in so many ways, but which on this occasion made him look as if I were stealing something from him, as though I were making away with the key to his office, for example. A look of vulnerability and defiance. A man threatened in his belly or somewhere, with the determination that I should *not* get away with it, I should *never* get away with it.

Thus the confused motives ("It is not our vocation to travel and attend meetings") become clear in ways other than words. (After all, our Father Chrysogonus is traveling all over the place, attending all kinds of things, and his stay in Europe has already been prolonged twice.)

Dom James regards this invitation to Collegeville as a personal threat to himself, to his prestige, to his very existence as father image and icon. If he were invited, he would probably attend. After refusing my Japanese permission, he himself took off for Norway. I am sure he is not aware of this himself. It appears to him only in the most acceptable terms. He thinks my humility would be deflowered by this meeting with experts, like Dom Leclercq. He detests Dom Leclercq, Dom Winandy, Dom Damasus Winzen and all these wicked Benedictines.

Well, I have to learn to accept this without resentment. Certainly not easy to do. So far, I have hardly tried, and to tell the truth, it angers and distracts me. So that is the vow of obedience. You submit yourself also to somebody else's prejudice and to his myths and to the worship of *his* fetishes.

Well, I have made the vow and will keep it, and will see why I keep it, and will try at the same time not to let myself be involved in the real harm that can come from a wrong kind of submission. There are several wrong kinds, and the right kind is not always easy to find.

In other words, I do not agree with those who say that *any* submission will do.

February 16

I must admit that over Sunday I was troubled by the whole business of that refused permission.

Father Abbot preached a long impassioned sermon on vanity, ambition, using one's gifts for one's own glory, etc., etc., on Sunday morning in Chapter, and I could see he was still very upset. There was a great deal of emotion. His voice was trembling in the beginning, his breathing was not altogether under control, and so on. Obviously this had something to do with my request. This is the way he usually operates and I thought it was quite unfair if it was.

I too was irritated and finally depressed, sitting there in a position of total helplessness and unable to respond or do anything about it. The feeling of powerlessness and frustration and most of all humiliation over the fact that I should feel it so much and be forced by my feelings to think about it all day. How absurd.

And yet the efforts I made to see it rationally, to see it as trifling and laughable, would not quite come off. Nor did the religious arguments and the repeated acceptance of it as a cross and humiliation in the depths of my will. Nothing seemed to make any difference, and finally I lay awake at night, the first time this has happened in the hermitage.

At last I wrote a note to Father Abbot saying I was sorry I had offended him, that his sermon had made me miserable but that my writing, etc., was not pure ambition and vanity, though obviously there was some vanity involved in it, and that I wished he would accept me realistically and not expect me to be something I can never be.

He replied that the sermon had had nothing to do with me, that he had no intention of hurting me, was most concerned, etc. Maybe it was an illusion, but anyway, there it was. I was relieved that it was all settled. A tantrum. I am surely old enough to be beyond that. (I don't really believe his reply.)

*   *   *

Yesterday, in the morning, when I went out for a breath of air before my novice conference, I saw men working on the hillside beyond the sheep barn. At last the electric line is coming. All day they were working on holes, digging and blasting the rock with small charges. Young men in yellow helmets, good, eager, hardworking guys with machines. I was glad of them and of American technology, pitching in to bring light as they would for any farmer in the district. And it was good to feel part of this, which is not to be despised but admirable, which does not mean that I hold any brief for the excess of useless developments in technology.

*   *   *

Afternoon. Landscape of stylites. The REA men all over the hillside, one on top of each pole. Brand-new copper wire swinging and shining, yellow hats all over the place. The light is coming.

1:30 p.m. They came in the morning and the first pole was already up by 9. I hope it may be finished by tonight. I was talking to some of them and they are real nice guys, open and friendly and without guile.

*   *   *

Evening. About 2:45, the red-faced foreman of the REA team, a very good simple man, came and set up my meter, and I put on the switch and had light. I was in the middle of translating some Pessõa poems for Suzuki in return for the calligraphy he sent me recently. The light is a great blessing.

The New Mexican mask at the end of the lattices shows up well and so does the black ink on Suzuki's scroll.

The icons look presentable, though they are much better in ordinary daylight, when the light is outside and they are in the shade of the room. An icon is meant to be seen in shadow and candlelight.

I celebrated the great event, the Epiphany and the coming of the REA, with a good supper of potato soup cooked on an old beat-up electric stove which Brother Joachim gave me. It works all right, so it is an evening of alleluia.

February 17

Early morning. I must admit that the light is a great help. It simplifies things. It makes prayer less complicated. There is no fussing with matches, candles, flashlight.

The electric heater is a help when the morning is not actually freezing, so that I do not have to light the fire and get into all the distraction of logs and pokers.

I am conscious of the fact that the light comes through others. I am part of a collectivity, a rural cooperative, the Salt River RECC. This is significant and consoling. In this light I am united to the people of the countryside who share the same source as I. But I am not on the same line as the monastery, which is on the big utility company, KU. I am with the poor farmers on REA.

*   *   *

I have been rereading the remarkable notes by S. in *La Vie Spirituelle* of 1952 on solitude. One thing I know now that I could not realize then. It is not enough to be a part-time hermit, living mostly in community, for he says: "Quand il faut composer entre les deux esprits, on partage ses forces entre deux tiédeurs" (When one has to compromise between the two spirits, one divides one's forces between two mediocrities). And this is perfectly true.

Hence I must keep working toward the day of a complete solitude, perhaps when I do not even go down to the conventual Mass. Still, I think it continues to make sense to take dinner down there so as to avoid the fuss of cooking. But as long as I am master of novices, I am obviously going to be tied down.

Father Flavian, my confessor, says it remains a duty of charity to be present with the community for at least a few things.

*   *   *

One of the things I liked about the REA foreman yesterday was that, after asking whether I saw a deer around here, he said, "I don't think I could ever kill a deer." And he said he thought probably a deer would come around here "because they know they would be safe." That was nice. But I told him that I had to chase hunters out of here all the time, even though it is supposed to be a wildlife refuge.

February 24

I have to go in to Dr. Scheen again today. The skin of my hands has erupted once more, leafed and cracked, and deep holes in the skin are quite painful. It interferes with work. Even tying shoes is painful. I had to wear gloves to make my bed. What a mess!

*   *   *

Brother Joachim was up yesterday to put some finishing touches on his electrical work and Brother Clement brought me a big glossy refrigerator which came Saturday, or was installed here that day. It immediately became a big distraction and in many ways I wish I did not have to have it, but in summer it will be necessary. The first couple of nights I was annoyed by the noise it makes when it wakes up to cool itself, and each time it did this, I woke up too. But I set myself to learn sleeping again and by the grace of God it worked. I might as well forget about being guilty, the thing is too splendid. But local people have such and they have TV too.

*   *   *

Everything about this hermitage fills me with gladness.
There are lots of things that could have been far more perfect

one way or the other, ascetically or domestically, but it is the place God has given me after so much prayer and longing and without my deserving it, and it is a delight. I can imagine no other joy on earth than to have such a place to be at peace in. To live in silence, to think and write, to listen to the wind and to all the voices of the wood, to struggle with a new anguish, which is, nevertheless, blessed and secure, to live in the shadow of a big cedar cross, to prepare for my death and my exodus to the heavenly country, to love my brothers and all people, to pray for the whole world and offer peace and good sense among men. So it is my place in the scheme of things and that is sufficient. Amen.

* * *

I am reading some studies on St. Leonard of Port Maurice and his *retiro* and the hermitage of the *incontro*. How clearly Vatican II has brought into question all the attitudes he and his companions took completely for granted, such as the dramatic barefoot procession from Florence to the *incontro* in the snow, the daily half-hour discipline in common, etc. This used to be admired, if prudently avoided, by all in the Church. This was thought to be "the real thing" even if only few could do it. Now we have come to be openly doubtful of the intrinsic value of such practices. The sincerity was there and it obviously meant a great deal to them, but depth psychology and so forth have made these things forever questionable. They belong to another age and to another kind of consciousness. They presuppose a certain unawareness of the unconscious. But it is in the unconscious that the true purification and repentance have to reach down and happen. Artificially austere practices have a tendency to prevent this deeper change. They can be a substitute for change in depth, although it is not necessarily true that they can *never* be associated with a deep change. But can they in our time?

Nevertheless, there has to be a certain amount of hardness, difficulty and rigor in the solitary life. The hardness is there all by itself. It does not need to be put there. The cold, the solitude, the loneliness, the labor, the need for poverty to keep everything simple and manageable, the need for discipline, for long meditation in silence; but no dramas, no collective exercises of self-chastisement, into which there can come so much that is spurious and questionable. Indeed, it is good to have a solitary life without this collective dimension. Even though it may be dangerous, it is better.

Evening of February 24

It has been a strange day. I end it by writing with dermal gloves on, as rain pelts down on the cottage.

I was supposed to go to town with Bernard Fox, but he had left when I arrived at the gatehouse at 8:03. As a result, while I was waiting for another ride, the brothers in the store were making signs to me. "It's a good thing that that fellow that wanted to kill you has gone away." Apparently, some nut in the guesthouse was breathing fire and brimstone on my account. In the mail too, there are some letters from some fanatics of varying degrees, who don't like me.

I rode into town with Bobby Gill, who is afraid to drive in city traffic and who, in fact, had never driven in Louisville before. He lives back in the woods the other side of New Hope in a little cabin with his family. He got me to the Medical Arts Building all right and slept peacefully in the parking lot while I was in the doctor's office.

The doctor does not know what is causing this dermatitis. He took bits of skin for a lab test. I wear dermal gloves. My hands *hurt*.

Riding back, about noon, we made good time. If I had been with Bernard and the others, it would have meant lunch in Louisville. As it was, Bobby Gill wanted only the sandwiches he had left from his job with Brother Christopher. I got some food at the supermarket in Bardstown and ate lunch at the hermitage.

Then at the end of the afternoon I went back to the monastery. I had a couple of direction sessions in the novitiate and went to the infirmary kitchen to stock up on sugar.

Over the public-address system from the Chapter Room, they were reading a stern reproof of the hermit life in a book by a Benedictine. Father Roger, who was standing there, told me that Brother Gerard had received the last sacraments at 6 p.m. and was very low.

Coming up in the rain, I thought peacefully of death and accepted the fact that very possibly some madman might come up here one night and do me in and, if that is the way it is to be, I am glad to accept it from God's hand. He will give me the grace to die pleasing to Him.

Bobby Gill is now living at the entrance to the back road that leads to Edelin's place. Bell Hollow is its proper name. Keith Hollow branches northeast from it. So, if I go to live in Bell Hollow, Bobby Gill could possibly be my contact man with the monastery.

Malcolm X, the Negro radical, has been murdered. I am sorry to hear it. Now there is fighting among different factions of black nationalists.

February 26

I see more and more that solitude is not something to play with. It is deadly serious, and much as I have wanted it, I have not been serious enough about it. It is not enough just to "like solitude" or love it even. Even if you like it, solitude can wreck you, I believe, if you desire it only for your own sake.

So I go forward, and I don't believe I could ever go back (even interiorly I have reached a point of no return), but I go on in fear and trembling and often with a sense of lostness, trying to be careful what I do because I am beginning to see that every false step is paid for dearly.

Hence, I fall back on prayer or try to. Yet no matter; there is great beauty and peace in the life of silence and emptiness. But to merely fool around with it brings awful desolation. When one is trifling, even the beauty of the life suddenly becomes implacable. Solitude is a stern mother who brooks no nonsense. And the question arises—am I so full of nonsense that she will cast me out? I pray that she will not and I suppose that is going to take much prayer.

*   *   *

I must admit that I like my own cooking. Rice and pinto beans today, for instance, with apple sauce from the monastery and some peanuts. A nice supper.

*   *   *

I read an excellent Pendle Hill pamphlet. Douglas Steere sent it. It is by Edward Brooke. Three letters on the situation in South Africa. They are hopeful in a Christian sense but I wonder if that hope will, in fact, be realized in history. Certainly it is important to understand South Africa if we want to get a real perspective on our own racial problem.

February 27
The solitary life makes sense only when it is centered entirely on the love of God. Without this, everything is triviality. Love of God in Himself, for Himself, sought only in His will in total surrender. Anything but this in solitude is nausea and absurdity.

But outside of solitude, one can be occupied in many things that seem to have a meaning of their own; and their meaning can be and is accepted, at least provisionally, as something that must be reckoned with until such time as one can come to love God perfectly. This is all right in a way, except that, while doing things theoretically "for the love of God," one falls, in practice, into complete forgetfulness and ignorance and torpor. This happens in solitude, too, of course but in solitude, where distraction is evidently vain, forgetfulness brings conscious nausea. In society, forgetfulness can bring a certain kind of comfort. It is therefore a great thing to be completely vulnerable and feel at once, with every weakening of faith, a total loss. In that way, one has to struggle against the weakening.

*   *   *

Things that in community are legitimate concerns are seen in solitude to be also temptations, tests and questionings. For instance, the skin trouble on my hand.

March 2, Shrove Tuesday
Light rain, Forty Hours [devotion]. A pleasant vigil last night with the novices in church. But it took a long time for the church to calm down after everyone had gone to bed. The sacristans were running around for half an hour.

*   *   *

I am reading a good biography of Simone Weil which I have to review for *Peace News* in London. I am finally getting to know her. I have a lot of sympathy for her, although I cannot agree with some of her attitudes and ideas.

Basically: I wonder what disturbs me about her. Something does. In her experience of Christ, for example: is it Gnostic rather than mystical? But, one has to admit, she seems to have seen this herself and she did not cling to what was wrong. "The attic" was a place she had to leave behind. Her mystique of action and the world is her true climate, now familiar and, I think, more authentic. For a time, I think Catholics were running to Simone Weil to learn this, but now they have forgotten and Teilhard de Chardin is the prophet of this cosmic Christianity.

(And yet, what about St. Francis?)

*   *   *

One thing the hermitage is making me see is that the universe is my home and I am nothing if not part of it. Destruction of the self that seems to stand outside the universe. Get free from the illusion of solipsism.

Only as part of the world's fabric and dynamism can I find my true being in God, who has willed me to exist in the world. This, I discover here in the hermitage, not mentally only but in depth and wholeness, especially, for instance, in the ability to sleep. At the monastery, frogs kept me awake. There are frogs here but they do not keep me awake. They are a comfort, an extension of my own being. Now the hum of the electric meter near my bed is nothing, though in the monastery it would have been intolerable. So there is an acceptance of nature and even of technology in my true habitat. I do not have to work the thing out *theoretically*. It is working itself out in practice in a way that does not need to be explained or justified.

March 3, Ash Wednesday

Though I may be uncomfortable with Simone Weil's imaginative description of her experience with Christ, I think her mysticism has something basically authentic about it. Though I cannot accept her dogmatic ambiguities, I think her reasons, her *personal* and subjective reasons for not joining the Church, are quite sincere. They are profound as well as challenging. Furthermore, I can also see that these might be from God and therefore they may have a special reference to the Church, a special relevance to the predicament of the Church in our time. They are perhaps a kind of accusation of the Church, an accusation which might be seen as coming indirectly from God Himself.

What does impress me in Simone Weil is her intuition of suffering and love: her insistence on being identified with the unfortunate and with the unbeliever. The realization that God's love must break the human heart.

And finally this: "Blessed are they who suffer, in the flesh, the suffering of the world itself in their epoch. They have the possibility and function of knowing its truth, contemplating its reality, its suffering of the world. But unfortunate are they who, having this function, do not fulfill it." Another quote: "We have to discard the illusion of being in possession of time." So says Simone Weil. And this implies consenting to be "human material" molded by time under the eye of God.

March 4

Simone Weil has to be taken as a whole and in her context. Individual and independent as she was, the whole meaning of her thought is to be found, not by isolating it, but by situating it in her dialogue with her contemporaries. The way to dispose of her uncomfortable intuitions is not to set her apart and look at her as if she were a totally isolated phenomenon. Her non-conformism and mysticism are, on the contrary, an essential element in our time. Without her contribution, we would be less human.

Take, for instance, the special importance of her critique of shallow personalism.

See also her prophetic remarks about the Americanization of Europe after the war, which would deaden the Oriental roots of contact with the East in Europe. Her intuition of America as purely non-Oriental and rootless. Her vision of a world threatened with rootlessness through Americanization. This is quite a thought. Consider the symbolic meaning of Vietnam and the burning Buddhists. South America (and this is my addition) is more Oriental as well as more European than North America and this is perhaps the hope of the world, a bridge, a remedy.

Simone Weil thought France should substitute cultural exchange for colonial domination.

She concludes that the exposure of America to the shock of misfortune may make America see the need for roots. But there are no signs of this so far!

*   *   *

Evening—lots of wet snow.

I had to spend the whole day in the monastery, as I had a conference, directions and so forth, and then in the afternoon a long meeting of the building committee (from which I wish I could decently resign) about the project for the new church.

I came briefly up to the hermitage after dinner to sweep, pick up the water bottle to refill and also to read a few pages of a new book, Nishida Kitaro's *Study of the Good*, which Suzuki sent and which is just what I am looking for at the moment. It is magnificent.

But the rest of the day was dreary enough—a test of patience and resignation. Really, I don't care too much. It was wonderful to get back to the hermitage and silence in the evening, to see the trees full of snow outside the bedroom window.

*   *   *

This morning, I said a Requiem Mass for Simone Weil and also spoke of her in the conference to the novices and juniors, reading Herbert's poem on love, which she liked.

*   *   *

The magazine *Holiday* paid me a thousand dollars for "Rain and the Rhinoceros," which they have changed into "The Art of Solitude." (Later, they changed it back to the original title.) Otherwise, there has been no editing except my own, though maybe they edited out the SAC plane. I must look again when the magazine comes. The galleys were here a few days ago.

March 5

Nishida Kitaro is just what I am looking for. For example, I see my objection to the cliché about "meaningful experience" as if it were meaningfulness that made experience somehow real and worthwhile. "Experience" is thought to be made "meaningful" by being referred to something else—a system, or perhaps a report of someone else's experience—and therefore its quality is diminished. So the ambiguity of "meaningfulness" is exposed. When experience becomes "meaningful," it also, in some sense, becomes unreal or less real. To live always outside of experience as if it were the fullness of experience! This is one of the basic ambiguities of Western thought.

*   *   *

A curious thing! Finishing the book on Simone Weil, I discover that it was Tom Bennett, my godfather and guardian, who tried to treat her in the Middlesex Hospital and had her transferred to Ashford because she refused to eat and rejected his care. Funny that she and I have this in common! We were both problems to this good man.

March 9

Several days of rain, mist, damp, cold.

It is flu weather and there is flu in the monastery.

A postulant left and another one came. This one was a Carthusian for a few months at Parkminster (which does not mean that *this* is the best place for him!). We had a meeting about him yesterday and decided to give him a chance.

Father Timothy is on retreat for diaconate, so I spend more time in the novitiate and it was pleasant being there yesterday for Lenten reading.

The place is quiet and peaceful—almost a hermitage itself.

It seems to me that since I have been more often in the hermitage the novices themselves have become much quieter and more serious. I have never done less work with them and never had them so good.

My conclusion is: there is much, too much, anxiety on the part of superiors to interfere with and "direct" their subjects.

*   *   *

Yesterday I sent off the review of the Simone Weil book to *Peace News* and finished some translations of a few poems of Nicanor Parra, who is excellent: sharp, hard, full of solid irony. He is one of the best South American poets, a no nonsense anti-poet with a deep sense of the futility and corruption of social life, a sense which has now been taken over entirely by poets and writers.

*   *   *

I sent the Pessõa poems to Suzuki. Dan [Walsh] said that he had read some of them to his class at Bellarmine.

*   *   *

The new Mass began Sunday and there are good things about it but it is obviously transitional. I will miss the prologue of St. John at the end of the Mass but I am saying it in my Thanksgiving. After all, that is what it was intended for, anyway. Actually, I did not realize how much this "Last Gospel" had drawn to itself and soaked up all the associations of all the joys of fourteen years of Mass and priesthood for me.

All those simple quiet Masses—nine years and more of them in the novitiate chapel. Summer mornings—saying the Last Gospel with the open window looking out toward the green woods of Vineyard Knob. The text itself is one of the most wonderful in the Bible. Certainly ideal for contemplation.

March 10

There is no question now that the Mass ends too abruptly. One has to go more slowly and deliberately, perhaps with a few discreet pauses, or one is suddenly unvesting, as it were, in the middle of Communion.

Of course, a whole new attitude toward the "shape" of the Mass is now required. This attitude is implicit in the new rite; but one must feel it and bring it out. One needs to see the Mass celebrated by priests who have thought out the new implications and experienced their meaning. So far, after all, it is only four days; we here seem to be dutifully setting out the bare fragments of a liturgy in a new arrangement, without having grasped the organic significance of what is going on.

*   *   *

After four or five grim, wet days, cold and dark, suddenly we have bright spring. Cold, clear blue sky with a very few, clean, well-washed clouds, thin and full of light. The wet earth is springy. Green moss shows in the short grass under the pines. The frogs sang for a moment, but it is still cold. The buds are beginning to swell. A flycatcher was playing in the woods near the stile, as I came up, and the pileated woodpecker, bright-combed, darted out, swinging up and down over the field to the east.

*   *   *

All day I have been uncomfortably aware of the wrong that is in me. The useless burden of pride I condemn myself to carry, and all that comes with carrying it. I know I deceive myself as a monk and a writer, but I cannot catch myself in the act. I do not see exactly where the deception lies. Perhaps it is a question of trying to do things that are beyond me, or trying to have something to say about everything. I do not have enough mistrust of my own opinion. Beyond that, there is my rebellious and nasty dissatisfaction with everything—with the country, with the Church, with the monastery, although not so much with the monastery now.

I am accepting it more peacefully and I see how foolish it is to rebel against what is, after all, human and normal and only to be expected. I am, unfortunately, very impatient with the uniformly benign, vague, public pronouncements of Pope Paul VI, as if he could be anything else. Perhaps he is trying earnestly to do something about Vietnam. I am impatient with biographies of new cardinals, read from the newspapers, in the refectory.

At the root of it all is a mean and childish impatience with myself and there is no way of dignifying it as a valid protest.

March 14, Second Sunday of Lent

The sense of wrong is still with me. I now see the negative and weak side of my intentions in writing *Seeds of Destruction*, an element that was invisible to me before, as if I wanted to make sure that I too was part of the human race and concerned in its concerns. Well, I am. There is nothing wrong with that. But for various reasons I do not understand, and because of all the usual ambiguities, I am too anguished and too excited, especially since I am out of touch with what goes on.

Because of this, the book, or at least the part on race, fails to make complete sense. It is not fully useful in the current situation. The part on war has, I think, greater value. The letters may, in some cases, be all right, but they also show the foolishness and futility I have got into with all my mail. Yet I cannot honestly say that I have wished this all on myself. The letters that come in *do* impose a certain obligation by themselves. I have to try to answer some of them and I have not, certainly, gone looking for them.

March 15

Yesterday afternoon it was cold and rainy. I read a little of Eric Colledge's essay on Mechthild of Magdeburg under the tall pine trees behind the hermitage before going in to shave and give my conference—the last conference on Ephrem—and then sing Vespers.

I love the Lenten hymns, all the hymns. What a loss it will be if they are thrown out.

In the evening it cleared, became cold. I came back up to the hermitage with the sun setting and the moon out. I looked out the bedroom window and saw two deer grazing quietly in the field, in the dim dusk and moonlight, barely twenty feet from the cottage. Once in a while, they would look up at the house with their big ears extended. Even a little movement would make them do this, but eventually I walked quietly out on the porch and stayed there and they remained peacefully, quietly, until finally I began moving about. Then they lifted up the white flag of their tails and started off in a wonderful, silent, bounding flight down the field only to stop a hundred yards away. I don't know what became of them after that, for it was my bedtime and I had not read my bit of Genesis (on Jacob's dream), so I read it and went to bed.

March 19, St. Joseph

Bright full moon, cold night. The moonlight is wonderful in the tall pines. Absolute silence of the moonlit valley. It is the twenty-first anniversary of my simple vows.

*   *   *

Last evening I was called over to the guesthouse for a conversation with Father Coffield, who is on his way back from the march at Selma and returning to Chicago. He is one who left Los Angeles in protest against Cardinal McIntyre.

He talked about the tensions and excitements of Selma, and described what it was like to be on the line facing the police at 3 a.m.

There was a legal and official march in Montgomery. Though everything is not yet over, there seems to have been a breakthrough, and the violence of the posse men seems to have had a great deal to do with bringing it about. The protest is going on all over the nation. It is very articulate, and Congress is intent on getting something done. This is due, in great part, to the fact that everyone saw everything on TV. From now on, I will be more careful about what I say against TV.

Father Coffield spoke of John Griffin, who has been very ill and is in the hospital again.

March 21, Third Sunday of Lent

On the afternoon of St. Joseph's, I went over to Edelin's valley with some novices and went to explore on my own a couple of thickly wooded hollows over the ridges south of Bell Hollow. They are both excellent snake pits and I would not want to go there in summer. Coming back over the ridge into Bell Hollow in very thick brush, I got hit in the eye by a branch of sapling. It wounded the cornea and, for two days, I have not been able to see properly out of that eye. It is only a little better today, though it hurts less, what with ointment and dark glasses.

I was able to do very little work yesterday except cooking, gathering wood, etc. I said Office and tried to read a bit with the left eye and wrote a letter to Nicanor Parra.

March 23

Hausherr remarks that in patristic times the theology of baptism was the theology also of Christian perfection, that is to say, it was spiritual theology. This is a more profound remark than it seems to be at first sight. By baptism, a man becomes another Christ and his life must be that of another Christ. The theology of baptism, therefore, teaches us who we are. The consequences are easy to deduce. The saint, or *hagios*, is one who is sanctified in the sense of sacrifice. Compare John 17:19.

In other words, martyrdom is the perfect response to the baptismal vocation. (Compare St. Ignatius of Antioch.)

At the same time, Origen, in the true spirit of non-violence, warns against the impure motive of self-love, which leads one to court death without consideration of the sin of those who would destroy us. We must also consider the importance of remembering the spiritual welfare of the persecutor himself. This has to be taken into account. The experience of the Deep South shows that the death of the martyr does not automatically redeem and convert the persecutor.

In any case, martyrdom can never be a mere improvisation. The only preparation for martyrdom is not some special technical training but the Christian life itself. Thus, eventually a truly Christian life, worthy to be consummated in martyrdom, is treated as almost equivalent to it. Then you get the ideal of the confessor and the monk. This is simply the life of true discipleship.

The mark of such discipleship is perfect love of the Saviour and of the Father's will. He who does not live according to his baptism and discipleship is living as a potential renegade from martyrdom.

*   *   *

My eye gets better only slowly. Ointments and even a black patch have been necessary for a couple of days. Only today am I able to read with it again and that makes it burn. But this has been a grace. I have been sobered by it. What was I doing charging through the woods on that godforsaken ridge? Trying to see if I would come out where I did. All right, but it was still useless. I would have been better off quietly praying, as I did yesterday afternoon in that lovely glen where I used to go twelve years ago.

I was preparing the sermon on St. Benedict, which I had to preach yesterday, and I was much struck by the idea of judgments of God. The thought took deep hold on me that what matters in our life is not abstract ideals but profound love and surrender to the concrete judgments of God. They are our life and our light. Inexhaustible sources of purity and strength, but we can ignore them, and this is the saddest thing of all.

March 23, Evening
My eye is slightly better but not yet healed.

There was a high wind all day. It is my free day at the hermitage and in the middle of the afternoon a knock came on the door. It was my neighbor, Andy Boone. He wanted to talk about the fence line he is working on and a deal about three white oaks he wants to cut down. He offered me twenty-five dollars a month to pasture his cows in the field next to the hermitage and I said no, on account of the locust seedlings we put in there last spring, and so on. One very good thing came out of it.* He told me there was an excellent spring that had got filled in and buried some years ago. It is only fifty yards or so behind the hermitage through thick brush. I knew the place and did not realize there was a spring there, though water is running there now. We will clear it and perhaps pump it to the hermitage. Anyway, clear it.

I went out there and saw a dozen places in the thick brush where deer had been sleeping. They are my nearest dormitory neighbors—thirty or forty yards from my own bed or even less. How wonderful!

*　　*　　*

Andy Boone was full of all kinds of information and stories. For one thing, he said that the water from all these springs comes from the Lake Knob. He was told this by a geologist. He had the geologist here looking for uranium!

He has a lot of stories about chasing people from Elizabethtown

---

*This was not a good thing at all. It was a very bad thing! As the results proved. T.M.

out of the woods when they come to have wild parties by night near Dom Frederic's Lake. He talks about hunters who are too lazy to get out of their cars and sit in them by the roadside, shooting woodchucks in our field. He tells how Daniel Boone first came to Kentucky and spread the people around wherever there was water and then went off himself to Indiana. In Indiana, he had a hole that he hid in when the Indians were after him. He withdrew into it, pulled a stone over it, and they never found him. The hole was eight miles long and twelve feet high and nine feet wide and had a stream in it, and when a powder plant was being built on which Andy worked before World War II, a bulldozer disappeared in this hole and that is how it was discovered.

All this is typical Andy Boone talk. Andy Boone is an old farmer who has been living here all his life on the farm next door to the property where I live. He is always around the monastery and knows a lot about the monks and has an inexhaustible fund of stories that only a madman would take seriously. I know what it costs to believe him!

March 26

Vile rain and fog.

I came up last night in very heavy rain with a cold beginning. As long as I stay in the hermitage and keep the fire going, the cold is not too bad. It was a bit bothersome in the community, where there is flu. The choir is overheated. You sweat and then get chilled. I wish I could simply stay up here at the hermitage and say Mass up here.

I have grapefruit juice in the icebox and that is a big help. I decided to take some bread with my coffee this morning instead of fasting on coffee only until dinner. The rye bread was good and so was the coffee.

*   *   *

Dan Walsh is giving his momentous talk at Catholic University today and I promised I would say a Mass of the Holy Spirit for the canonization of Duns Scotus. His talk is ostensibly about Duns Scotus and Anselm but also, and above all, consists in the development of his own ideas on the metaphysics of faith. I shall be very interested to hear it when he gets back.

*   *   *

Evening. The weather continued to be very foul all day. It is plague weather. I have not been able to see across the valley all day long. My cold is a little worse, but not much.

I sat out the conventual Mass alone in the back of the brothers' choir and could see a few good fathers look back disapprovingly from the monks' choir, as if there were a divine commandment to sit with the other invalids in the transept when you have a cold. Actually, it was quite impressive to follow the Mass from back there—a thing I had never done before. The main reason I was there was to be completely alone. I suppose that is what everybody resented.

*   *   *

After I got back to the hermitage, Andy Boone came by with a check for a hundred and twenty-five dollars for the trees he cut down on the fence line and he talked some more. Am I going to be in perpetual conversation with this man? He was talking of the connection of dogwood trees with the passion of Christ. And one of his favorite topics—how to tell the sex of cedar trees. Only the "she trees" make good Christmas trees, he says. He claims that our planting loblolly seedlings brought in the beetles which are killing cedars and Virginia pines. This I can well believe.

March 27

The moon is out, the sky is clearing at last. The air is drier and fresher. There is a very thin film of ice on the water buckets. Last end of the old moon. The new moon will be the moon of Easter.

March 29

The hope of better and drier weather died quickly yesterday. The sky darkened and at night there was thunder, lightning, heavy rain beating down and, half awake, I remembered that I had left my rubber boots down at the house and thought of my cold, which gets no better. Fortunately, I had a raincoat at the hermitage.

The fire alarm at the monastery went off at about 5:30 and the rain abated, so I went down. It was a false alarm. Water got into the warning system. It kept on raining all morning.

Then I received an anonymous letter from Alabama from a reader who desired to prove her sincerity by saying she was a mother and grandmother and who said my book *Seeds of Destruction* was appalling, spelled "appauling." Some clippings from the Alabama papers were enclosed. Nothing but righteous indignation and outrage. In fact, the same irrationality, the same ferocity that one saw in the Nazi press twenty years ago. One theme only—that some degraded and despicable people, "outside agitators," were simply defiling, insulting and gratuitously provoking the good people of Alabama; that such things were simply beyond comprehension and beyond pardon; that the thought of considering any apparent reason behind them was totally unacceptable; that Alabama had done and could do no wrong. Complete failure to face reality.

Another murder took place last week after the Montgomery marches.*

March 31

Better weather yesterday.

My biggest distraction these days is Andy Boone, who extracted from me a vague agreement that he ought to cut down some oaks at the top of the field east of the hermitage. His sons have been out there with chain saws making a frightful racket and sending the biggest white oaks (naturally) crashing down one on top of the other. By last evening, the woods were in a fine mess, with one big tree hung up in another and a third hanging on the one that is hung up. I persuaded him yesterday to direct his attention elsewhere and cut up the dead trees around the spring so that we can get in there and clean it up.

But my cold is better and I am trying to get back into some serious meditation. Serious, not just hanging around quietly and

---

*That was probably the murder of Viola Liuzzo. T.M.

moodily. Here too, there is a spring to be cleared and I am not going deep enough these days.

April 3

This morning I finished the appendix to Nishida Kitaro's *Study of Good*, which gives some idea of the full scope of Nishida's thought. It is most satisfying. Happily, there is at least one other of his books in English. The *Study of Good* is his first. The development from here is not linear, but a special deepening of his basic intuition of pure experience, which becomes "absolute nothingness as the place of existence," and "eschatological everyday life," in which the person as a focus of absolute contradiction (our very existence opening onto death is a contradiction) can say with Rinzai, "Wherever I stand is all the truth." This hit me with great force. My meditation has been building up to this. (Awareness, for instance, that doubt arises from projection of the self into the future or from retrospection and not grasping the present. He who *grasps* the present does not doubt.)

To be open to the nothingness which I am is to grasp the All in whom I am.

*   *   *

Yesterday I marked the trees that Andy Boone is to cut down and I have to see that he cuts down *only* the trees that are marked. They are all in the hollow behind the hermitage, where the spring is. What a tangle of brush, saplings, vines, fallen trees and honeysuckle! Marks of deer everywhere. A fire in there would be a disaster. I hope we can get a space of an acre or so good and clear between here and the spring and keep it clear and I can use the spring, for I need it.

All this wild area is the geographical unconscious of my hermitage. Out in front, the conscious mind, the ordered fields, the wide valley, tame woods. Behind, the unconscious, this lush tangle of life and death, full of danger, yet where beautiful beings move, the deer, and where there is a spring of sweet pure water buried.*

---

*It is sobering to reflect that the spring was not so pure! T.M.

April 4, Passion Sunday

Light rain all night.

The need to keep working at meditation and going to the root. Mere passivity won't do at this point, but activism won't do either. A time of wordless deepening to grasp the inner reality of my nothingness in Him, who is.

Talking about it in these terms is absurd, nothing to do with the concrete reality that is to be grasped and is grasped. My prayer is peace and struggle in silence, to be aware and true, beyond myself. To go outside the door of myself, not because I *will* it but because I am *called* and must respond.

April 6

Tuesday in Passion Week.

A rainy, humid, stuffy day—as warm as summer. Had to go to town to see the eye doctor. My eye is still injured by that blow I got from the branch in the woods on March 19. I saw Dr. Flowers. It is the first time I have been in the new Medical Towers near all those new hospitals, which have so transformed Gray Street from the lazy Southern street it was ten years ago.

The windows of the Presbyterian Seminary are boarded up. The seminary has moved out of the old fake-Gothic building, Scotch Victorian Tudor or whatever it was. They are now up by Cherokee Park.

So I sweated in the doctor's waiting room and read copies of *Life* magazine—one more tedious than the other. Great emphasis on the mess in Vietnam, trying to make it look good, honest, reasonable, and so forth, which it is not.

Senator Cooper gave a good speech in the Senate against extending the war and I got a letter from him in reply to one I had written about it. He seems serious and sane about it.

April 9, Feast of Our Lady of Sorrows.

Friday in Passion Week.

Dawn is beginning (5:30) on a mild spring morning. Holy Week is about to open and I was never more conscious of its solemnity and its importance. I am a Christian and a member of a Christian community. I and my brothers are to put aside everything else and recognize that we belong, not to ourselves, but to God in Jesus Christ, that we have vowed obedience that is intended to unite us in Christ, obedient unto death, even the death of the cross. That, without our listening and attention and submission in total self-renunciation and love for the Father's will in union with Christ, our life is false and without meaning.

But insofar as we desire with Christ that the Father's will may be done in us as it is in heaven and in Jesus, then even the smallest and most ordinary things are made holy and great. Then, in all things, the love of God opens out and flowers. Then our lives are transformed. This transformation is an Epiphany and advent of God in the world.

It is unfortunate that so much of monastic obedience has become merely formal and trivial. There is no use in lamenting this, but nevertheless, renewal in this area must mean, above all, a recovery of the sense of *obedience to God in all things* and not just obedience to rules and superiors when obedience is *demanded*: and after that, go wool-gathering where you may!

A sad thing that formal obedience or non-disobedience is an expedient which, in practice, justifies us in self-will in harmless and futile matters. Thus our lives, in fact, become totally absorbed in futilities, which are licit and which are not subject to formal control. Instead of imitating Christ, we are content to parody Him.

One of the fruits of the solitary life is a sense of the absolute importance of *obeying God*, a sense of the need to obey and *to seek His will*, to choose freely, to see and accept what comes from Him, not as a last resort, but as one's daily supersubstantial bread. This means liberation from automatic obedience into the seriousness and gravity of a *free choice to submit*; but it is not always easy to see where and how.

April 13

Tuesday in Holy Week.

On Palm Sunday, everything was going well and I was getting into chants of the Mass when suddenly the Passion, instead of being solemnly sung on the ancient tone in Latin, was read in the extremely trite and pedestrian English version that has been approved by the American bishops. The effect was, to my mind, complete bathos, a total lack of nobility or of solemnity or of any style whatever. It became an utterly trivial act. I could not get away from the impression of a comedy. Not that English is not capable of serious liturgical use, but the total lack of imagination, of creativity, of any sense of worship in this pedestrian version! Yet many in the community were delighted, including the professor of liturgy.

*   *   *

In the evening conference, I talked (foolishly) of Angela of Foligno and then back to Philoxenos.

After supper and direction, I went up to bed in the hermitage feeling unwell. I woke up after an hour's sleep with violent diarrhea and vomiting, which went on for most of the night. Fortunately, the night was warm and moonlit. I was weak and nauseated all yesterday. I began to feel better in the evening and took a little supper. I slept last night in the infirmary and slept well too. Had a good breakfast of fried eggs and coffee. I felt a little weak this morning, but on the whole I seem to have got off easy, unless it starts up again after supper, which I suppose it might. While it lasted, it was a miserable experience.*

April 15, Holy Thursday
Obedient unto death.

Perhaps the most crucial aspect of Christian obedience to God today concerns the responsibility of the Christian, in technological society, toward creation and God's will for his creation. Obedience to God's will for nature and for man; respect for nature and love for man; awareness of our power to frustrate God's designs for nature and for man, to radically corrupt and destroy natural goods by misuse and blind exploitation, especially by criminal waste.

The problem of nuclear war is only one facet of an immense complex question.

*First indication of what was in the water of the "pure" spring. T.M.

A theologian writes: "It is the duty of the Christian to lead the world of nature to its natural perfection." And this is true in a sense, but it is written with a tone and with implications that are perhaps misleading. It assumes that technology is obviously doing something to perfect nature; it does not consider that technology might be squandering and abusing nature in the most irresponsible fashion.

There are then very grave problems in the implications of a certain kind of Christian outlook on the world. The crux of the matter seems to be to what extent a Christian thinker can preserve his independence from obsessive modes of thought about secular progress, behind which lies the anxiety for us and for the Church to be acceptable in a society that is leaving us behind in a cloud of dust.

In other words, where is our hope? If, in fact, our hope is in a temporal and secular messianism of technological and political progress, we find ourselves, in the name of Christ, joining in the stupidity and barbarism of those who are wrecking his creation in order to make money or to get power for themselves. But our hope must be in God.

* * *

Yesterday I got out of the infirmary at my own request, perhaps too soon, but I felt better and wanted to get back to the hermitage, though it tires me to come out here.

Last night I was restless and feverish, sweating a lot, and had to change my shirt three or four times. At the end of the night, I had some rather beautiful dreams and got up at three. My meditation wasn't much good, as I was feeling sick. But some superb tea that Jack Ford gave me, Lapsang Souchong, made me feel much better. It is the most effective medicine I have taken in this sickness, a marvelous tea. That, with a slice of lemon and a couple of pieces of rye toast, made a fine breakfast, and after reading a bit, I am very alert and alive. But as heavy rain began about 4:30, I did not go down to the monastery for Chapter and some of the ceremonies.

The rain is slowing down now at 7:15. The valley is dark and beautifully wet. You can almost see the grass growing and the leaves

173

pushing out of the poplars. There are small flowers on my redbuds and the dogwood buds are beginning to swell.

There is no question for me that my one job as a monk is to live this hermit life in simple direct contact with nature, primitively, quietly, doing some writing, maintaining such contacts as are willed by God and bearing witness to the value and goodness of simple things and ways, loving God in all of it. I am more convinced of this than of anything else in my life and I am sure it is what He asks of me. Yet I do not always respond with perfect simplicity.

April 16, Good Friday

Today, God disputes with his people. One of the rare times when he argues with man, enters the court and pleads his own cause. O my people, what have I done to you? Man blames God for evil, but it turns out that all the evil in the world has been done through man by the mysterious adversary of God. And all the evil has been done *to* God. He who need not have taken it upon Himself has done so in order to save man from evil and from his adversary. The adversary, and man allied with him, makes himself "be" by declaring himself to be real and God less real or unreal, trying to reduce God to nothing on the cross. But God, the abyss of being beyond all division of being and nothingness, can neither be made to be nor reduced to nothing.

The judgment: those who have turned their hate against God have in reality destroyed themselves in striving, in their own manner, to assert themselves. The way to "being" is then the way of non-assertion. This is God's way. Not that He has a way in Himself, but it is the way He has revealed for us, revealing Himself as the way. "I am the way," said Christ. And last night we went out of Chapter into the church for concelebration.

April 17, Holy Saturday

The great sin, the source of all other sin, is idolatry and never has it been greater, more prevalent, than now. Yet it is almost completely unrecognized precisely because it is so overwhelming and so total. It takes in everything. There is nothing else left.

Fetishism of power, machines, possessions, medicines, sports, clothes, etc., all kept going by greed for money and power. The bomb is only one accidental aspect of the cult. Indeed, the bomb is not the worst. We should be thankful for it as a sign, a revelation of what all the rest of our civilization points to. The self-immolation of man to his own greed and his own despair. And behind it all are the principalities and powers whom man serves in this idolatry.

* * *

A warm bright spring day. I saw a palm warbler in the small ash tree behind the hermitage with his red-brown cap and bobbing tail. He is on his way to the north of Canada. Why do they call him a palm warbler?

April 18, Easter Sunday

The peace and beauty of Easter morning! Sunrise, deep green grass, soft winds, the woods turning green on the hills across the valley and here too.

I got up and said the old Office of Lauds and there was a wood thrush singing Fourth Tone mysteries in the deep ringing pine wood, the unconscious wood behind the hermitage. (The unconscious wood has a long moment of perfect clarity at dawn. From being dark and confused, lit from the east, it becomes all clarity, all distinct, seems to be a place of silence and peace with its own order and disorder. The fallen trees don't matter. They are part of it.)

Last night I went down to the Offices of the Easter Vigil by full moonlight, the woods being perfectly silent and the moon so strong one could hardly see any stars. I sat on the porch to make my Thanksgiving after Communion. I did not concelebrate, I only went to Communion.

April 19, Easter Monday

The study of medieval exegesis is a way of entering into the Christian experience of that age, an experience most relevant to us, for if we neglect it, we neglect part of our own totality. But it must not be studied from the outside. The same idea in Nishida on Japanese culture and the Japanese view of life.

I have a real sense, this Easter, that my own vocation demands a deepened and experiential study from within of the medieval tradition as well as, to some extent, of the Asian tradition and experiences, particularly Japanese and particularly Zen, i.e., in an awareness of a common need and aspiration with these past generations.

April 23, Easter Friday

It is already as hot as summer. Everything is breaking out into leaf and the pine sawfly worms are all over the young pine trees. There is no visitation this year. (Dom Columban usually comes for the visitation of the monastery on Easter Friday. He comes from our Mother House in Melleray in France.)

This year the General Chapter opens next week and Dom James is to leave Sunday.

This morning I sat in the dentist's chair having my teeth cleaned and X-rayed while the students banged and walloped next door, demolishing the old library.

Early mornings are now completely beautiful with the Easter moon in its last quarter, high in the blue sky, and the light of dawn spreading triumphally over the wide cool, green valley. This is the paradise season.

*   *   *

I was deeply moved by Tertullian. What magnificent Latin and what a concept of the dignity of man and of the body! See his treatise on the Resurrection, chapters 6 and 7.

Yesterday, Flannery O'Connor's new book [*Everything That Rises Must Converge*] arrived. I am already well into it. It is grueling and powerful. A relentlessly perfect writer, full of tragedy and irony. But what a writer! and she knows every aspect of the American meanness and violence and frustration: above all, the Southern struggle of will against inertia.

*   *   *

A pine warbler was caught in the novitiate scriptorium beating against the window and I got a good look at him, letting him out. A couple of towhees are always busy near the hermitage.

April 25, Low Sunday

I wonder if the singular power of Flannery O'Connor's work, the horror and fascination of it, is not basically religious in a completely tacit way? There is no positive and overt expression of Catholicism. Certainly no expression of religious optimism and hope, but perhaps a negative, direct, brutal confrontation with God in the terrible and in the cruel. For example, see the bull in the story "Greenleaf," as the lover and destroyer. This is an affirmation of what popular Christianity always struggles to avoid at all costs: the dark face of God.

But now and above all, in the South, it is the dark and terrible face of God that looks down upon America. The crazy religious characters are to be taken seriously precisely because their religion is crazy and inadequate.

*   *   *

5:40 a.m. Thunder over the valley. Fork lightning and very black rain out there beyond the monastery. And all the birds sing, especially a wood thrush in a cedar tree. Rain begins to come down on the hermitage.

April 27

I have been thinking about the ideas which Dom James may or may not have about Bell Hollow and which he may express, perhaps even at the General Chapter, for which he left early Sunday. He refuses to say anything explicit about it. I know he wants to start something there, but more and more I feel repugnance and misgivings about the way it seems to be planned.

For example: a group of people living in trailers, with compact comforts and modern conveniences. Certainly, this is practical, and he is thinking of his own desire to live there himself. But that is simply what I need not seek. All in all, I become more convinced that I am much better off in the hermitage where I now am. I am resolved not to get involved in any plan of Dom James' that is to be worked out over in Bell Hollow.*

* * *

Today for the first time since Passion Week—that is to say, for three weeks—I have some news of what has been going on in Vietnam. Things are incomparably worse. Though there was a big demonstration for peace in Washington on Holy Saturday and though the State Department, evidently at Johnson's request, wrote a conciliatory note to the FOR [Fellowship of Reconciliation] about their big protest ad; though the South Vietnamese and especially the Buddhists are desperately trying to get a government that will be more independent of the Pentagon and more representative of all —more open to the idea of peace—still the bombing of North Vietnam gets heavier and heavier. Thousands more American troops are going to be sent over. Johnson says he wants peace, and every time he says it, he escalates the war. His only concept of peace is to have the "enemy" flat on his face in front of him, in unconditional surrender, asking only to be dictated to by American power.

It gives a strange and forbidding idea of what we have slowly become in this country: this, and all the other things: the fat Mississippi sheriffs grinning into the camera, knowing they can murder people and get away with it; grave questions about the murder of President Kennedy (which the Warren Commission never really explained); the country full of kooks and Birchites—not to mention the others. Suddenly we begin to look like the Nazis, the impossible ones, the morally dead in a landscape of damnation. What can anyone do about it? That is the question.

Most people in the country seem to have no conception that this is taking place. They simply believe what they are told and they cannot be blamed for doing so. How should they know better?

---

*In actual fact, it was at this General Chapter that Dom James put up a very strong plea for allowing hermits in our order and, against a certain amount of opposition, put it across because of his own desire to be a hermit in Edelin's valley. As a result of the General Chapter officially approving hermits, I myself was officially allowed to leave the community in August 1965 and live completely as a hermit. T.M.

They trust the media and the official sources of information without realizing how much these are giving them a doubtful and distorted picture of what is actually going on.

* * *

I received a copy of Jacques Maritain's *Notebooks* from Paris and have already read the interesting and sometimes funny chapter on La Salette: concerning his attempts to get his manuscripts about the apparitions approved in Rome in 1918.

There are some very fine pages on the nature of prophetic language, the language of heavenly revelations. What comes out most of all, of course, is the simplicity and probity of Jacques himself, and his obedient loyalty to the Church. It is very edifying.

I love the pictures of Raïssa and Vera [Maritain]. Though I never actually met them, I know they are two people who loved me and whom I have loved through our writings and the warmth and closeness that has somehow bound me to Jacques and to them. It is really a kind of family affection, which also reaches out to good Dom Pierre Van der Meer, who wrote recently about the article concerning La Pira's visit here—and his somewhat enthusiastic account of his stay at Gethsemani.

May 1
Perfectly beautiful spring weather. Sky utterly cloudless all day. Birds singing all around the hermitage. Deep green grass.

When I am here all the time, the towhees and tanagers are at peace, not worried. And with their constant singing, I always know where they are. It is a wonderful companionship to have them constantly within the small circle of woods which is their area and mine, where they have their nest and I have mine. Sometimes the wood thrush comes but only on very special occasions, like the evening of St. Robert's day.

Last evening, I interrupted my meditation to watch a half-dozen Savannah sparrows outside my bedroom window.

* * *

Today I finished a first draft of an article on contemplation and ecumenism for a Dominican magazine in California.

A copy of the *Black Revolution* in Catalán came in. This has appeared in the following languages and in this order: one, French; two, English; three, German; four, Catalán!

*   *   *

Rumors are going around the monastery about trouble in Santo Domingo. Johnson has sent in American troops. It seems to be another pretext for escalation of war.

Today I read a Xerox of Herman Kahn's article on "Escalation" from a recent issue of *Fortune*. It is fantastic. His peculiar vocabulary gives it a bizarre, comic quality. A parody of technological think-tank double-talk could hardly be more strange. There have come into being in our time new idioms that cannot be parodied: they are parodies of themselves. But this is not funny: far from it, very serious indeed, all the more so since Kahn is close to speaking the mind of Pentagon officialdom in many respects. Or he certainly has a following there, among whom his word is Gospel.

The dispassionate, "scientific" lingo of games-theory war! At no point does Kahn suggest that the megadeaths he plays with might involve *people*. Mass murder is simply a language, a means of bargaining: the vernacular of military wheeler-dealing. You evacuate a city. You take out two of the enemy's cities—like pawns in a game. You put down chips, you pick up cards, and you keep a poker face while fifty million of your citizens go up in smoke to prove you mean business, that you are a sharp cookie, that you know how to play nuclear poker.

And of course the game gets very interesting: "slow motion counter property war," "constrained force reduction salvo," "constrained disarming attack" building up to "slow motion countercity war," in which the game takes on something of the allure of a striptease, a tantalizing way to divest the map, bit by bit, of its populations. "City trading." Such fun! It is a nice "test of nerves," too, he reminds us.

He wants to sell us his toy. All this is perfectly "thinkable" and anything that is thinkable to Herman ought to be O.K. with the generals and with everybody else too. It may make some people vomit, but they have weak, unscientific stomachs, that's all.

What counts of course is *control*. As long as it is all *controlled*, then there is no problem, it is rational, scientific, efficient, therefore (set your mind at rest) it is *moral*. As long as it does not reach the last, unpermissible step of "spasm or insensate war," it is "controlled" and moral. This will be enough to pacify the scruples, if any, of most Catholic moral theologians. The moral theology of hell! (As if the war in Vietnam were not already "insensate.")

His plea is that there "has to be an alternative between cataclysm and surrender." Has he ever heard of making peace?

My conclusion from this article is that Washington is about to start climbing Herman's ladder, and to do it in short order, confident that Russia will understand and play along according to the most esoteric rules. I have no doubt whatever that this article was read with close attention in the Kremlin.

May 10

Already a most beautiful week of May has gone by. For part of it I was ill with the same bug that put me in the infirmary after Palm Sunday. This time I finally got an antibiotic that seems to have cleared it up. Last time it stayed with me and I could not get rid of it.

James Laughlin was here last Monday (May 3) and on Tuesday we went over to see Victor Hammer—a pleasant drive, and I took a few pictures of old barns.

On our way back, we stopped at Shakertown, which is now cleaned up and to some extent open to the public. But there, though I enjoyed the big sunny rooms full of that lovely furniture, I was already getting sick again with my bug. By the time we got to Bardstown, I wasn't enjoying things any more and my supper upset me.

Yesterday, the third Sunday after Easter already, is one of my favorites. The afternoon was warm and glorious with new summer, the brand-new summer and wheat already tall and waving in the wind and great cumulus clouds and all the things one cannot begin to say about it. The new awareness: that I am not the "object" that "they" think, or even that I think; and that the I is not I-all and in everyone; and that the outer-I must not assert itself anymore, but must be glad to vanish; and yet there is no division between them, as there is no division between the surface of the pond and the rest of it. It is the reflections on the surface that seem to give it another being.

There is an owl in the wood, something like a whippoorwill, which says, "Where's the widow? Where's the widow?" and he says it repeatedly, in a very peremptory way.

May 11

If I were more fully attentive to the word of God, I would be much less troubled and disturbed by the events of our time. Not that I would be indifferent or passive, but I could gain the strength of union with the deepest currents in history, the sacred currents which run opposite to those on the surface a great deal of the time.

May 15

A busy week. Yesterday, Father Xavier Carroll and Edward Noonan, a Chicago architect, were here. The abbess of the Poor Clares in Chicago wanted them to discuss with me the plans for their new monastery, which, in fact, looks quite attractive and which involves some big changes in their approach to the contemplative life.

Thursday, Sister Luke was here and we talked about the revised schema for religious, which, as a Council observer, she had obtained from one of the bishops but not from an American bishop.

Wednesday, I had a short visit with Dom Philip, Benedictine prior of Vallyermo in California. He had some good encouraging things to say about monasticism in Africa and about the group on the island in Lake Kivu (Africa), which sounds fine.

*   *   *

It is not altogether easy to make an act of faith that all of history is in God's hands—not at this point and on the level where I have just been standing, the level of current opinion, where history is thought to be made by President Johnson and his advisors and the Pentagon!

But history *is* in the hands of God. The decisions of men, however disastrous, lead infallibly to the full expression of what is really hidden in ourselves and in our own society. Our choices may be very idealistic—or appear so—but their real significance is shown by their results.

The actions of the United States in Asia are God's judgment on the United States. We have decided that we will police the whole world by the same tactics as used by the police in Alabama—beating other people over the head because we believe we have a right and a duty to do so since they are inferior. In the end, an accounting will be demanded.

We have to see history as a book that is sealed and opened only by the Passion of Christ. But we prefer to read it from the viewpoint of the Beast. We look at history in terms of hubris and power—in terms of the Beast and his values. Christ continues to suffer his passion in the poor, the defenseless, and his Passion destroys the Beast. Those who love power are destroyed together with what they love. Meanwhile, Christ is in agony until the end of time.

May 20

Paschal time is going by fast. We are in the fourth week of it already. There was more rain the other evening and everything is very green.

For once, the contradictions in my life, which do not usually bother me, are suddenly painful and I see I must really do something about them. For example, the question of having so many visitors. I cannot completely stop all visits, but I must cut down on them in some way—all except for a few that will remain really necessary and far apart.

May 22

Gray dawn, and a blood-red sun furious among the pines. That damn black hound is baying in the hollow after some rabbit he will never catch. Deep grass in the fields, dark green English woods (for we have had great rains). The bombing goes on in Vietnam. I wonder if the whole thinking of the country about war is not completely crazy: based on the myth of force. That only force can be effective, that violence alone "works" and that nothing else is "serious." That it is perhaps not "nice," but one must be realistic and resort to it—but to do so with moral justification, so as not to be mere gangsters, as "they" are. For "they" are obviously wrong and we are obviously right, since God is on our side.

So we are determined to take care of our affairs by force, because in the end force is all we believe in. Can a war with China be avoided? Perhaps if China keeps *extremely* cool. All we need is another Pearl Harbor, and if one comes, I will not be surprised.

May 23, Fifth Sunday after Easter
One lovely dawn after another. Such peace! Meditation with fireflies, mist in the valley, last quarter of the moon, distant owls. Gradual inner awakening, centered in peace, thankfulness, harmony, unity. I wrote to the man at McGill who thinks contemplation is "regressive." That is just what it is not. It is, on the contrary, complete awakening of identity, unity, rapport: not submersion, but full awareness of one's place in the whole: first the whole of creation, then the whole plan of Redemption. To find oneself in the great mystery of unity and fulfillment which is the Mystery of Christ. *Consonantia*, not *confusio*.

May 25
I went down to the monastery only for Mass, and came back up without going to vote in the county elections. (Why should I? I know nothing about these people.)

Jack Ford brought me a couple of loaves of pumpernickel from a Jewish delicatessen in Louisville and some fine tea, Twining's Earl Grey. I had both for supper, together with a small can of mandarin oranges. Cool and pleasant.

For meditation—I spent part of the morning on the Sapiential Books and then in the evening took the Apocalypse in Greek, as I have been doing lately. I have a good little book on Camus for light reading, and have just finished volume one of de Lubac's *Exégèse Médiévale*. Tomorrow, Vigil of the Ascension, is the sixteenth anniversary of my ordination. I will offer Mass for Vo Tanh Minh, who has been fasting in Brooklyn since March in protest against the war. He could starve to death and it would mean nothing whatever to anyone in Washington.

May 28
Cool and lovely morning, clear sky, every changing freshness of the woods and valley! One has to be in the same place every day, watch the dawn from the same window or porch, hear the selfsame birds each morning to realize how inexhaustibly rich and diverse is this "sameness." The blessing of stability is not fully evident until you experience it in a hermitage.

May 30
Wonderful days. Bright, cool weather. Clear skies and green hills.

Today I have finished my draft of Chuang Tzu poems, if one can call them that. More exactly, I finished them yesterday afternoon and went over them all this morning around dawn. I was exhilarated by the cumulative effect. They make a good group and I never would have thought it possible for the result to be so (relatively) satisfactory.

I am glad John Wu kept insisting that I do this job. It has taken a long time, but most of the time was spent just getting around to doing it. At first, I was very slow and hesitant, progress was painful. Lately it has been a lot of fun.

*   *   *

The flycatchers, tamer and tamer, play about the chairs and baskets on my porch right in front of this window. They are enthralling. Wrens come too but less frequently.

*   *   *

My stomach is still upset. It has not been the same since April. Next Friday I have to go to Lexington for X-rays.

*   *   *

They are still reading the life of Newman by Meriol Trevor in the refectory and I never get tired of it. My admiration for Newman grows constantly, the more I know the details of his life and all the nonsense he had to suffer from almost everyone and especially from the hierarchy of the Church. With what good sense and patience he took it after all!

June 3

I finished [writing] the introduction to *Chuang Tzu* this afternoon.

It is hot and misty. There is thunder in the distance. A cardinal sings in the quiet evening.

Dan Berrigan was here Monday with Jim Douglass and Bob McDole. We talked a bit about Schema 13 and the alterations that have been made in the article on war. It seems that some of the bishops want to officially approve the bomb after all. In a way it is funny, though I should not say that, but behind it all I wonder if there is not an apocalyptic irony. Still, we must do what we can to prevent a disgrace and a scandal of such magnitude.*

June 6, Pentecost

On Friday, I went to Lexington for examinations at the clinic of Dr. Fortune. I was supposed to return that afternoon but stayed overnight in the hospital for more tests yesterday morning. What with enemas, proctoscopes, barium enemas, etc., I had a miserable time. When I began these examinations ten or fifteen years ago, they were unpleasant but bearable. Since then, my insides have become so sensitive, they are a real torment. However, there is no cancer and there are no ulcers, just an enormous amount of inflammation and sensitivity. The results of all the tests are not yet in.

The usual hospital images and confusion. I am glad I got out so soon.

In the clinic, I seemed to be able to get hold of nothing but *Life* to read and it was full of helicopters in Vietnam, white mercenaries

---

*Actually, what we had feared did not take place and the Constitution was quite clear against the bomb. T.M.

in the Congo and Marines in Santo Domingo. The whole picture is one of an enormously equipped and self-complacent white civilization in combat with a huge sprawling colored and mestizo world, which is the majority, armed with everything they can lay hands on.

The implicit assumption behind it, as far as *Life* and apparently everyone else is concerned, is that "we" are the injured ones. We are trying to keep peace and order and "they," abetted by Communist demons, are simply causing confusion and chaos with no reasonable motives whatever.

Hence, we—being attacked and God and justice also attacked in us—have to defend ourselves, God and justice, etc. Dealing with all these inferior peoples becomes a technical problem, something like pest extermination.

In a word, the psychology of the Alabama police becomes, in fact, the psychology of America as world policeman. There is a world revolution going on in which now whole nations, whole races are involved.

Some of these nations are the rich and the aristocratic—and all the rest are the poor. Russia is in a very ambiguous position, as a rich nation that still claims to be on the poor side but isn't. America is oversimplifying all the questions, reducing them to terms which make sense to us only and to no one else, and expecting others to see things our way, since our way is, by definition, the only reasonable one. Hence, a fatal breakdown of communication, which is the worst problem today.

*　　*　　*

Wives of astronauts talk by radio with their husbands in outer space.

A priest of St. Meinrad's in Peru can call Jim Wygal and talk to him on the phone he has in his car while he is driving around Louisville. And what do they have to say? Nothing more than "Hi, it's a nice day, hope you are feeling good, I am feeling good, the kids are feeling good, the dog is feeling good," etc.

*　　*　　*

Coming home from the hospital in Lexington through Shakertown, Harrodsburg, Perryville and Lebanon: beautiful June countryside, deep grass and hay, flowering weeds, tall cumulus clouds, corn a foot high and beautifully green, tobacco struggling to begin. The old road between Perryville and Lebanon, winding between small farms and old barns with wooded knobs nearby, is one I like very much.

After Lebanon, we ran into thundershowers, heavy rain and black sky over the fields to the north, with much lightning. Country people in the streets of Lebanon on Saturday afternoon. It was a nice ride.

*   *   *

Coming through Pleasant Hill without stopping, I saw new aspects of the wonderful old Shaker houses. The inexhaustible variety and dignity in sameness! The old Shaker colony at Pleasant Hill, just this side of the Kentucky River gorge, is a place that always impresses me with awe and creates in me a sense of quiet joy. I love those old buildings and I love the way the road swings up to them. They stand there in an inexpressible dignity, simplicity, and peace under the big trees. They are completely empty now. There have been no more Shakers there for a long time.

June 8

The great joy of the solitary life is not found simply in quiet in the beauty and peace of nature or in the song of birds or even in the peace of one's own heart. It resides in the awakening and the attuning of the inmost heart to the voice of God—to the inexplicable, quiet definite inner certitude of one's call to obey Him, to hear Him, to worship Him here, now, today in silence and alone. In the realization that this is the whole reason for one's existence.

This listening and this obedience make one's existence fruitful and give fruitfulness to all one's other acts. It is the purification and ransom of one's own heart that has been long dead in sin. This is not simply a question of existing alone, but of doing with joy and understanding "the work of the cell," which is done in silence, not according to one's own choice or to the pressure of necessity, but in obedience to God, that is to say, in obedience to the simple conditions imposed by what *is* here and now.

The voice of God is not clearly heard at every moment; and part of the "work of the cell" is *attention*, so that one may not miss any sound of that voice. What this means, therefore, is not only attention to inner grace but to external reality and to one's self as a completely integrated part of that reality. Hence, this implies also a forgetfulness of oneself as totally apart from outer objects, standing back from outer objects; it demands an integration of one's own life in the stream of natural and human and cultural life of the moment. When we understand how little we listen, how stubborn and gross our hearts are, we realize how important this inner work is. And we see how badly prepared we are to do it.

June 11

Tomorrow, Fathers Timothy and Barnabas are to be ordained priests. I shall concelebrate with Father Timothy on Trinity Sunday. He has been the most competent and reliable of all my undermasters in the novitiate. Already Father Abbot is speaking of sending them to Rome this year and getting them ready quickly for the Norway foundation. We are to vote on the Norway foundation this morning in Chapter.

There is a certain amount of misgiving in the community about this, naturally. It is a risk, and Dom James is so obviously enthused by it that he is pushing ahead fast with the delight of the operator who has got a good thing going. It is a good thing in many ways. We have possible support in Norway from the Cistercian Bishop of Oslo, Bishop John, and all his friends, but more men are leaving here and we are shorthanded. Few novices come. Spencer is going to have to close down at least one recent foundation. Perhaps they will close the one in Chile. I hope they don't close Snowmass.

*   *   *

I take great delight in a book I borrowed from Victor Hammer when I was at the hospital, *The Tao of Painting*, a deep and contemplative book. I am reading it slowly with great profit. The author, Mai-Mai Sze, is becoming one of my secret loves.

I am discovering Ambrosian chant. Maybe the various lesson tones of Ambrosian rite may turn out to be very great aids to Lectio

Divina. For instance, the marvelous proper tone for singing readings from Genesis. I may try this. I notice, after practicing the Genesis tone, that it sounds quite Oriental.

I read a bit of a Syrian of the ninth century, Youssef Vousnaya, on humility, and it had extraordinary depth and resonance. Chanting gets these things from the head down into the heart—the hesychast idea! It makes one's inmost center resound with the truth conveyed, instead of merely registering it in the reason.

er Saturday

. The trees of St. Ann's wood are barely visible across flycatcher on a fencepost appears in momentary flight, sudden indecipherable ideogram against the void of anishes.

sides of the house: the gossip of tanagers. The two operate on the porch scuttle away when I arrive, however, from outside; but when I come from inside the house, I may move briskly, they are not afraid and stay where

*   *   *

To be conscious of both extremes of my solitary life, consolation and desolation, understanding and obscurity, obedience and protest, freedom and imprisonment. In one sense, I am transcending the community: in another, I am banned from it. In one sense, I am being rewarded, and in another, I am being punished or put under restraint. For instance, I cannot go to Asia to seek at their sources some of the things I see to be so vitally important—the Zen ground of all the dimensions of expression and mystery in the brushwork of Chinese calligraphies—painting, poetry and so forth. This is an imprisonment which I accept with total freedom. Whatever I need will be brought to me here but, nonetheless, it is an imprisonment and a confinement. And it is so intended by my abbot.

Doubtless, this can be seen as a perfecting of my monastic life and also as a final disillusionment with monastic life. It is a renunciation of meaningful action and protest in contemporary affairs. Awareness that the action itself may be ambiguous. The renunciation of action may be more clear and a better-defined protest than that given by the action itself.

I have no doubts and no hesitations about not being any part of the Norway project, which passed yesterday with very few black votes. Yet I can see where, in other circumstances, I could get totally and fruitfully involved in it. I know it is much better not to, however. For instance, there would be the ambiguous situation of being a famous convert, of making friends with Bishop John's artistic crowd at Oslo and all that. Better to stay out of it. And obviously, that is one of the things that the abbot would want to keep me out of and therefore he would never send me to Norway.

I protest by obeying, and protest most effectively by obeying in an obedience in which I am not subject to arbitrary fancies on the part of authorities, but in which I and the abbot are aware, or think we are aware, of a higher obligation and a demand of God: that my situation has reached this point is a great grace.

Some will say it has come to this perversely, through my own fault. To say this is to see only those "reasons" one chooses to see. This is not hard to do. It is done all the time.

June 14

Two concelebrations, one for Father Timothy's first Mass yesterday, another for Father Barnabas today. Probably the best concelebrations we have had here so far. They were very spirited and joyful. One felt that all the concelebrants were really in it with all their heart. I certainly was.

*   *   *

Bright fine weather. I cleaned out the closet where I keep the typewriter and paper. I typed the Origen poem which I wrote some time ago. I found a fine Ambrosian *Sanctus*.

*   *   *

Dr. Fortune sent the results of my tests in the hospital, which showed a staphylococcus infection in my intestines. I have been taking an antibiotic for three days and it seems to be helping quite a bit. This infection is obviously due to some water I drank from the spring behind the hermitage. The water was tested and found to be polluted.

June 18

Corpus Christi was yesterday. I did not concelebrate. It was a good cool day. I wrote to Marco Pallis in answer to a good letter of his about my own letter to Lord Northbourne. John Wu wrote and sent some chapters of his new book on Zen.

I corrected the proofs of the article on eremitism, which is coming out in the magazine of the order, though I would have preferred otherwise. I do not want to appear to publicize solitude in the order, still less to be crusading for it. Quite the contrary. It is best that people in the order do not become excited about this issue. They will only make another problem out of it.

Nevertheless, since Father Abbot has apparently come out strongly in favor of the hermit life in the General Chapter, and since the General Chapter has approved hermit experiments in the order, the editors of the magazine are very anxious to publish my article at the present time.

*   *   *

"Solitude" becomes for me less and less of a specialty, more and more just "life" itself. I do not seek to "be a solitary" or anything else, for "being" anything is a distraction. It is enough to "be" in an ordinary human mode with one's hunger and sleep, one's cold and warmth, rising and going to bed, putting on blankets and taking them off. I had two blankets on last night. It is cold for June.

Making coffee, then drinking it; defrosting the refrigerator, reading, meditating, working (I ought to get to the article on Symbolism today) and praying.

I live as my fathers have lived on this earth, until eventually I die, Amen.

There is no need to make a special assertion of my life or to declare it as "mine," though it is doubtless not anybody else's. I must learn to gradually forget program and artifice. I know this at least in my mind and I want it in my heart, but my other habits of awareness (awareness of accidental and trivial things) remain strong.

June 22

A misty morning. Lots of noise from Boone's cows.

Fathers Timothy and Barnabas are going to Rome, perhaps the first of September. This means a change of undermasters in the novitiate and I am trying to persuade Dom James to get a new novice master at the same time. He is reluctant, for no very solid reason. He insists that I wait until January—that is "better psychology," and so forth.

There is a fantastic picture of one of our astronauts in space over the curve of the earth and the North American continent with the Gulf of Mexico beneath him. An exciting achievement! No denying the greatness of this achievement: though it is useless, perhaps it has something of the uselessness of great art. Who knows? In any event, I see there is no sense in remaining blind to it.

To be aware of all this space-age business is to realize the tremendous symbolic importance of it, whether for good or evil I don't know, and maybe this is not for me to judge. There is simply the fact of such happenings, and of all that goes into making them possible.

I am hugely impressed too by the enormous gantries of Cape Kennedy and the astounding room where the instruments show where the space flight is going. No question of the marvelousness of all this. Does it have to be necessarily the greatness of the Beast? I don't think so. Whether or not it is, there is no sense in reviling it. So perhaps I, too, will become cool like everybody else.

June 26

The other day after Mass I suddenly thought of Ann Winser, Andrew's* little sister. She was about twelve or thirteen when I used to visit Winser at his parents' parsonage on the Isle of Wight. I remember that quiet rectory in the shady valley of Brooke. She was the quietest thing in it. A dark and secret child. One does not fall in love with a child of thirteen and I hardly remember even thinking of her or noticing her, yet the other day I realized that I

*A school friend in England. T.M.

had never forgotten her and that she had made a deep impression.

I was left the other day with a sort of Burnt Norton feeling about the part of the garden I never went to. A feeling that if I had taken another turn in the road, I might have ended up married to Ann. Actually, I think she is a symbol of the true (quiet) woman with whom I never really came to terms in the world, and because of this, there remains an incompleteness in me that cannot be remedied.

When I came to the monastery, Ginny Burton remained as the symbol of the girl I ought to have fallen in love with but didn't and she remains the image of one I really did love, with a love of companionship, and not of passion.

*   *   *

There is now more of a possibility that the change in the novitiate may be made in September and I may be able to move out entirely to the hermitage then.

Reading Karl Stern's *Flight from Woman*, I find some fascinating material, especially in the chapter on Descartes.

*   *   *

Back to the picture of the astronaut "walking" in space, which is now in color on our cloister notice board. Space flights are, after all, a rather expensive way of convincing oneself that one is free from a mother. I see the beauty of the uselessness—and its utter uselessness. This space business will certainly never get anywhere, or not to any other "where" that they may be thinking of. It will have momentous results, but how and in what? I don't think anyone yet really knows. But for me, precisely, what matters is not space but earth.

The Bible spoke of paradise as the beginning, the harmony of heaven and earth, of father and mother, not of man coming down from a heaven of ideas in outer space. What are we trying to find? What number? Who are we trying to contact out there?

The real importance of Teilhard is his affirmation of the "holiness of matter" and this is the real reason why some Christians are shocked by him. But I do not oppose him on this ground (matter equals mater equals mother). My own opposition is to naïve Teilhardism and not to Teilhard himself. I have not studied him enough but I find him, personally, a very sympathetic figure.

June 28

Brother Job has made some "wine," which is not bad but certainly not as strong as he claims. Brother Clement is still in Europe.

The Critic has asked for an article on existentialism and I think I will write it.

June 29

Yesterday, after my Mass, I was distracted, as I am more and more lately, by the fear that in an abbatial election I might be elected abbot. I certainly do not think this fear is entirely irrational, though perhaps it disturbs me too deeply. In any event, no election is imminent here!

If I were elected, I would certainly refuse. But the distraction begins here. Supposing for some reason I *could* not refuse. Suppose it were forced on me. In the first place, I don't think it can be forced on anyone, but anyway suppose it is. It is at this point in the distraction that I find myself overwhelmed with temptations to depression and despair. I can hardly imagine a more impossible situation among those that are likely to happen in my life as it is now.

First, I am profoundly disillusioned with the Cistercian life as it is now going. I am certainly willing to obey those who claim to be running it, but to run a community myself would be inconceivably absurd. I have no interest in the aims that would have to be mine if I were abbot. I would not want to let the monks down, but how could I possibly do anything for them and how could I handle all the misfits and malcontents in the monastery except by throwing them all out? But you can't just fire non-adapted monks.

It seems to me that if I took on the job, within three years the monastery would be in a state of collapse, but I think I would probably collapse myself in three months. That is the way this distraction goes. It causes me much anguish.

Finally, at the conventual Mass, I was moved by the Gospel and the Introit: "When you are old, they will bind you and lead you where you do not want to go." I was able, at least, to accept the idea in peace. Supposing the job were really obviously God's will. I would try to take it in a spirit of trust and faith and forget myself. But, in any case, I think my vow would be respected and I have no real fears. This interior surrender brought me real peace. What matters is not the job or the refusal but simply God's will and His ways. His love is enough.

*   *   *

Another painful situation is coming up with Dom James. The board of editors of the *Collectanea*, the magazine of the order, is supposed to meet in Belgium in September. I am on this board and they want me there, since the magazine is in crisis. Well might it be. It is not a very good magazine. So, though I have told the editor what the situation is, he is still intent on getting me there. Dom James will undoubtedly do everything he can to prevent my going by fair means or ——. He is not always scrupulously fair in such matters. And the emotionalism, the illuminist arguments he will put forward!

I dread having to talk about it with him. However, I may not even be involved in the mess. He may squash the whole thing in a five-page letter to the Abbot General and there will not even be any discussion on my part. Well, perhaps that is best. One simply can't talk rationally to the man on such issues. There is no communication with him.

But meanwhile Brother Clement has been in Europe for two months. He has finished his business in Norway a month ago. Others have had their leave extended over again, and so on.

*   *   *

I got down to the monastery to find a vituperative letter of a postulant whom we rejected in December, accusing us of unfair treatment, saying that we gave him the bum's rush, etc. Considering this letter, I am very glad we did reject him. Also, the other day, I got a letter from a paranoid, who writes frequently.

I was glad to get back to the healing silence of the hermitage, the tall pines in the hollow where Brother Colman and the novices have been cleaning out the pine tops left by Andy Boone after his messy logging operation last Lent.

Not all was bad in the monastery, however. There was a good letter from Donald Allchin at Pusey House at Oxford and a good sermon on the missions by Father Romanus.

June 30

Hot damp weather, as befits this season. Yesterday was hot and quiet and there was a succession of thundershowers. One at dinnertime, one in the early afternoon, one toward suppertime. The second was the longest and best. Many clouds and the heavy downpour. It filled all my buckets with washing water. During part of the time, Andy Boone was up here trying to get leave to cut some more pine trees and telling all sorts of old stories about the old days, about water witches and gold diviners. (He had a gold diviner here who could seem to divine nothing but Fort Knox!) He also talked about Civil War guerrillas, about the great strength of our former Brother Pius, about the monks mining iron from Gap Hill to make bolts for the first building, and so forth.

Andy Boone is someone whose statements are not to be taken seriously. I know this to my cost, after believing him about that spring. I also refused him any permission whatever to touch a tree in our woods here.

After supper I went down to the monastery and took my turn on the night watch. I came back in a dark summer woods with a few fireflies. At night, there was another storm, but I barely heard it.

July 5

Does my solitude meet the standard set by my approaching death? No, I am afraid it does not. That possibility that is most intimate, isolated and my own, cannot be shared or described. I cannot look forward to it as an experiment I can analyze and share. It is not something to be understood and enjoyed. To "fully understand" and objectively contemplate death beforehand is a real imposture. But the solitary life should partake of the seriousness and incommunicability of death, or should it? Is that too frigid and too absolute an ideal? In any case, the two seem to go together. Solitude is not death, it is life. It aims not at a living death but at a certain fullness of life. Yet it is a fullness that comes from honestly and authentically facing death and accepting it without care, that is to say, with faith and trust in God. Not with any special social justification, not with any reliance on some achievement which is approved or at least understood by other people. Unfortunately, even in solitude, though I try not to and sometimes claim not to, I still depend too much emotionally on the idea of being accepted and approved and of having a place in society. But obviously there is no such thing as an absolute solitude. Even my solitude is my place in society. This solitude is, to some extent, recognized: but even if it is not recognized, it remains a "place."

Now it is true that in my life the witness of solitude may perhaps be significant, but there is danger here. This is one of the points where I see my own defenselessness, my weakness, my capacity to pretend, my tendency to be untrue to myself. I must learn to face my untruth in solitude, in preparation for the awful experience of facing it irrevocably in death with no more hope in anything earthly, only God. I must learn to do this without appealing to others for reassurance that I am not so untrue after all. How do they know one way or the other? What can they tell me? We are all equally sinners, all equally in need of God's mercy. They cannot justify me any more than I can justify myself.

Certainly, enough is evident merely in this Journal to destroy me forever after I am dead. But that is the point—not to live as one who can be so destroyed. This means not ingenuously discovering infallible ways of being "true" in the eyes of others and of posterity, if any, but of accepting my untruth and the untransferable anguish that is characteristic of death, and leaving all justification to God alone. Everything else is nothing but wrath, flame, torment and judgment.

The greatest comfort is to be sought precisely in the Psalms, which face death as it is, under the eye of God, and teach us how we may also face it. They bring us, at the same time, into contact or rather communion with all those who have so seen death and accepted it before us. Most of all, the Lord Himself, who prayed the Psalms on the cross.

July 9

From the way Dom James now talks, it seems he will be willing to make the change of novice masters* when Father Timothy goes to Rome in September, in which case I will probably be in the hermitage for good and will begin my real adaptation to solitude. Even sleeping here is only a halfway solution. To finally cut the tie with the community with no job and no official place in it, this will be momentous for me. Then the whole question of mail, of publication, and so forth, arises but I think this will solve itself.

* * *

My one real difficulty with faith is in really accepting the truth that the Church is a redeemed community, and to be convinced that to follow the mind of the Church is to be free from the mentality of the fallen society. Ideally, I *see* this, but in fact there is so much that is not "redeemed" in the thinking of those who represent the Church.

To my mind, the idea of officially approving the bomb in Schema 13 is not exactly a convincing demonstration of holiness and of guidance by the Spirit. I wonder what they will really do. Actually, I must do much more praying and thinking about the question of the Church to see it more in depth than I do. Certainly, I cannot accept a merely individualistic Christianity, that is to say, seeing the feasibility of an authentic Christian life for individuals but not for the Christian community. On the other hand, too external a view of the Church would be quite wrong. Who really is the Church, this "spouse of Christ, so bright and clear"? Well, the Catholic Church, but then ———?

What about the life of Newman, which still goes on in the refectory? It is so inexhaustibly important and full of meaning for me. Look what the hierarchy did to him! The whole thing is there existentially, not explicit, but it is there for the grasping. The reality is in his kind of obedience and his kind of refusal. Complete obedience to the Church and complete, albeit humble, refusal of the pride and chicanery of churchmen.

*Looking back, I am quite convinced that one of the main reasons why Dom James consented so easily to let me go to the hermitage at this time was that this was the best way for him to cut short all arguments about going to the meeting of the editors of the magazine in September. T.M.

July 14

A very busy day. In the afternoon, Jim Douglass with his wife, Sally, and Father John Loftus came out from Bellarmine College. We went up to the lake and sat under the young pine trees and drank Cokes. Some local kids were swimming in the lake. It was cloudy but did not rain until suppertime.

Jim says there is much talk that Pope Paul may come to the UN this September. I gave him copies of La Pira's letters to Robert Kennedy. La Pira is working earnestly for disarmament, but there is not much sign of this country disarming. The Vietnam war has shown the complete stupidity of Johnson in a way that everyone can see except the average American. Jim says the polls are running 70 percent in favor of the war. That is all that matters to people like Johnson.

I came back to the hermitage not feeling like going to bed. Mist over the field after rain, diffuse sound of crickets in the dusk.

I sat on the porch and the strange cry of a frightened deer came from the field. I saw the white tail bounding away in the mist. Nine o'clock now rings. I had better think of going to bed.

July 18, Sunday

There is a special peace and sense of blessing on Sunday morning, though all mornings are equally quiet here at the hermitage and the same birds always sing. This special peace is sensible even when there are no signs of Sunday such as the faint Mass bell from the village church in New Hope, far across the valley. Today the peace is even greater because of the storm and cleansing during the night. A very violent thunderstorm broke out about one, with continual lightning and uninterrupted thunder for almost an hour. I slept through one of these a few weeks ago, but not this one. Lightning touched the riser of my electric system and was grounded, but I felt the click of it through the whole house and even felt as if electricity were coming out of my feet in bed.

*   *   *

I see more and more that my understanding of myself and of my life has always been most inadequate. Now that I want more than ever to *see*, I realize how difficult it is. Though there is danger, doubtless, in solitude, I realize more than ever that here, for me, is confrontation with the word and with God and with the only possibilities that are fully real; or, at least, with those that are most real for me. Obviously, there is much that is real in the community, but more and more, as I go down there, I have the sense that reality is smothered there and words are substituted for reality. Yet my job and that of the Church remain this: to awaken in myself and in others the sense of real possibility, of truth, of obedience to Him who is holy, a refusal of pretenses and servitudes, without arrogance and pride and without any specious idealism.

July 19

A big jetliner coming down toward Louisville in the dawn sky. A beautiful great fish with an enormous tail fin and a long body which, at one moment only, caught itself under the clear bronze gold glint of sunrise. Then it slid on down behind my black pine trees.

* * *

Father Abbot said yesterday that on August the 20th, the feast of St. Bernard, he would make the changes in the novitiate and I would thenceforth be free to live in the hermitage all the time, with no further responsibility except to give one conference a week, in the novitiate, on Sunday. Father Baldwin is to be the new novice master. Father Timothy will go to Rome soon after that.

This was a very pleasant surprise and I was most happy about it. Very moved and very grateful. Things like this make me ashamed of my fears and worries and my suspicions.

Concelebration after that was moving, humbling and a consoling experience. I think I will have no more of my foolish feelings about concelebrations. Thank God for enough light to see my childishness.

Afternoon in the very quiet hollow behind the hermitage, the "unconscious" wood. I studied a few sayings of the Desert Fathers, thinking seriously about the change that is to come and is so momentous for me. One of the great mercies of God in my whole life and the answer to so many prayers.

Yet one sees here that everything has been really leading directly to this, even when it appeared to be hopeless. How happy I am that I stayed on the path where I was all along and did not succeed in getting off it, though, by God's grace, my efforts to get off the path were just what kept me most truly on it. And if I had not tried to go elsewhere, I would certainly not be in this hermitage now. I do not propose this as a working formula for everybody, however.

July 20

Great peace for the last couple of days since the decision. Any day one could write: "great peace"; but this is a very special and new dimension of peace, a tranquillity that is not got by cultivation. It is given and "not as the world gives, do I give unto you." The peace is not "it," but confrontation with "thou." Here, Buber is certainly right. Confrontation with Thee in this world of solitude all because of this one word yesterday. All is unified by this. One will, one command, one gift. A new creation of heavenly simplicity.

"If a man hears Tao in the morning and dies in the evening, his life has not been wasted." I think I begin to see what this means.

July 21

Went in to see Dr. Ryan. Actually, things had already begun to get a little better and he relieved the discomfort considerably. I had a certain amount of free time and read a good article on ecology in *Daedalus*. The day and the drive were pleasant.

As usual, the only darkening came from the news magazine in the doctor's office including an appalling rape case in *Newsweek* some weeks ago in Los Angeles.

The Vietnam war is generally taken for granted, though there is some vocal opposition. The war is tragic in Vietnam itself, and the war mentality here is nonsensical, complacent, vulgar, morally illiterate.

Actually, most of the news is no news at all. It is fabricated— or else the usual score sheet (sheer guesswork!). So many of ours dead, so many of theirs estimated dead. Estimated because our side drops tons of bombs on wide areas of jungle and hopes somebody will get hit. Or else we bomb cities in North Vietnam. Well, not yet cities as such, but targets which may be in or near them. The turn of cities as cities will eventually come. The news reports read now like those in nine months of World War II.

July 25
Very hot Friday and Saturday. The first really oppressive summer weather we have had in this extraordinary season.

Last evening I was too torpid to pray seriously but hung around trying nevertheless. I made orangeade for supper and put it in the freezer, thereby accidentally discovering how to make rather good sherbet.

Storms all night after eleven. I slept through most of it. They still continue now, halfheartedly, in the morning at 7:15. Since it rains, I do not go down to Prime but will go down later for con-celebration.

July 27
I finished the first draft of my article on existentialism for *The Critic*. Thank God I have that out of the way. Now I have nothing else to do but set things in order, clear out a lot of books, and get ready to move entirely out of the novitiate on the 20th of August.

July 28
I have to go into the hospital for a checkup before entering the hermitage.

August 6
Returned to the hermitage today after a week in St. Anthony's Hospital. In a way it was trying, at least, a test of patience. I had to rest, take medicine and sit in a room with machinery going outside and with an air conditioner on day and night. The even noise of the air conditioner neutralized the heavy traffic on Barret

Avenue and I was astonished to find myself sleeping nine hours a
night in spite of it. Evidently, it was something I needed—that
and the diet.

My stomach finally calmed down. I suppose I enjoyed it in a
way. I got some work done. Finished the galleys of *Seasons of
Celebration* and made a few new additions. I tried to keep my
presence there quiet, but Dr. Bizot was lector at my Sunday Mass.
He and Jack Ford came in, also Dr. Roser.

Today I drove home with Jim Wygal through winding county
roads, Taylorsville, Bloomfield, after having dinner with him at the
Old Stone Inn. It was awfully good to get back to the silence of
the monastery and especially to the hermitage, freshly painted by
one of the novices.

Two weeks until the big change.

August 10

The solitary life, now that I really confront it, it is awesome,
wonderful, and I see I have no strength of my own for it. Rather,
I have a deep sense of my own poverty and, above all, an awareness
of wrongs I have allowed in myself together with this good desire.
This is all good. I am glad to be shocked by grace, to wake up in
time and see the great seriousness of what I am about to do. Perhaps
I have been merely playing at this; and the solitary life is not
something that you can play at. Contrary to all that is said about
it, I do not see how the really solitary life can tolerate illusion or
self-deception.

It seems to me that solitude rips off all the masks and all the
disguises. It tolerates no lies. Everything but straight and direct
affirmation or silence is mocked and judged by the silence of the
forest. "Let your speech be yea, yea." The solitary life is to stand
in truth; hence the need to pray, the need for theological food, for
the Bible, for monastic tradition. The need to be entirely defined
by a relationship with and orientation to God my Father; that is
to say, a life of sonship in which all that distracts from this relationship is seen as fatuous and absurd. Above all, the work of hope
and not the stupid, relaxed, self-pity of acedia. Great need to honor
God by personal truth in the personal grace of solitude.

A beautiful poem of Tung Shan, which I find in John Wu's Zen manuscript:

For whom have you stripped yourself of your gorgeous dress
The cuckoo's call is urging all wanderers to return home
Even after all the flowers have fallen, it will continue its call
In the thickets of the wood among the jagged peaks.

August 14
Yesterday I was busy most of the day trying to clean out the novice master's office, to sort out what to keep and what to throw away. When I did get up to the hermitage, for part of the afternoon, Brother Clement showed up and stayed about an hour talking about his European trip.

The insane accumulation of books, notes, manuscripts, letters, papers in the novice master's room simply appalls me. Trying to sort it out upsets my stomach.

August 17
Yesterday I finally finished cleaning out, sorting, and throwing away manuscripts, notes, letters, and so forth. I wonder how many wastepaper baskets I have filled in the last week. And with this absurd ritual of wastepaper has gone a rending of the intestines.

August 18
Yesterday morning, there was a meeting of the Private Council to vote approval of Father Baldwin as the new novice master. Then I went out and they voted on my retirement to the hermitage. The vote was favorable (in fact, unanimous).

August 20
In Hebrews 11, after speaking of all the faith and suffering of former saints, the writer concludes: "All these who have borne witness to the faith did not receive what was promised because

God foresaw something better for us, that apart from us they should not be made perfect."

Entering upon my new way, I think especially of this: that I form part of the promise and fulfillment for which many others have suffered and hoped and, in my turn, I will suffer and hope and prepare the way for others still. In leaving immediate contact with the community and with society, I enter into this other close-knit society of invisible witnesses and I'm very aware of their presence.

August 21

Yesterday, I gave my final official conference as novice master and left the novitiate. The day was cool and peaceful. But still there were things to be done at the last minute, like transferring my alb and so forth to the library chapel for Mass, getting a hook in the washroom over in that building, writing and receiving farewell notes, making arrangements about clothes, and so forth.

* * *

This morning, gray, cool peace. The unquestionable realization of rightness of what I have done. This is from God and it is his work. What is immediately perceptible is the immense relief. The burden of ambiguity is now lifted and I am without care. I have no more anxiety about being pulled between my job and my vocation. I feel as if my whole being were an act of thankfulness. Even my gut is relaxed and at peace after good meditation and a long study of a book on St. Irenaeus.

August 25, Feast of St. Louis

The five days I have had in real solitude have been a revelation, and whatever questions I may have had about it before are now answered. Over and over again, I see that this life is what I have always hoped it would be and always sought. It is a life of peace, silence, purpose and meaning. Certainly it is not easy. It always calls for a blessed and salutary effort, but a little of this goes a long way. Everything about this life is rewarding.

My stomach trouble has cleared up. Everything is falling nicely into place. One can live at a good, quiet, productive tempo. Manual work in the morning, writing in the afternoon. Plenty of time for reading and meditation. And I notice that my reading schedule automatically simplifies itself and I want to spend more time on one thing only. The desperation and agitation of those old days are settling of their own accord. Already the novitiate life is becoming incredible. My last months there were not reasonable and the change is welcome.

Of course, I remember the novitiate of two, five and eight years ago as more real. In my first year as novice master there was a strain—as if I were playing some role I really did not want to play.

Now I am getting down to the business of meditation and total silence. I realize how little I really desire or need to simply talk to anybody. Certainly, not for talking's sake.

It is good to go at least for whole days without speaking, without really seeing anyone except my Mass server, and a few monks encountered on the way to Mass or in the infirmary refectory.

September 1

September has come in a great downpour of rain. It began about suppertime last evening and has continued on and off all night. It was especially heavy around 4:15 a.m. when I went out and looked at it and listened to it. Rain creates a double isolation and peace in the hermitage. The noise of it and the thickness of it walls you off from the rest of the world and you know that no one is going to bother to walk up through the woods with all this water coming down.

September 6

Magenta mist outside the windows. A cock crows over at Boone's farm.

Last evening, when the moon was rising, I saw the warm burning soft red of a doe in the field. It was still light enough, so I got the field glasses and watched her. Presently a stag came out of the woods and then I saw a second doe and then, briefly, a second

207

stag. They were not afraid. They looked at me from time to time. I watched their beautiful running, their grazing. Every movement was completely lovely, but there is a kind of gaucheness about them sometimes that makes them even lovelier, like adolescent girls. The thing that struck me most—when you look at them directly and in movement, you see what the primitive cave painters saw. Something you never see in a photograph. It is most awe-inspiring. The *muntu* or the "spirit" is shown in the running of the deer. The "deerness" that sums up everything and is sacred and marvelous.

A contemplative intuition, yet this is perfectly ordinary, everyday seeing—what everybody ought to see all the time. The deer reveals to me something essential, not only in itself, but also in myself. Something beyond the trivialities of my everyday being, my individual existence. Something profound. The face of that which is both in the deer and in myself.

The stags are much darker than the does. They are mouse-gray, or rather a warm gray-brown, like flying squirrels. I could sense the softness of their brown coat and longed to touch them.

INDEX

INDEX

INDEX

211

INDEX

Rawicz, Piotr, 36–7
Raymond, Father, 138
REA, 106, 115, 117–18, 149–51
Reardon, Father Barnabas, 189, 191, 193
Regan, Father Shane, 78
Reinhardt, Ad, 8, 69, 141
Reinhold, Father H. A., 9, 72
Rinzai, 169
Roberts, Archbishop T. R., 51, 113
Rochester, 68, 75
Roger, Father, 138, 153
Romanus, Father, 197
Rome, 9, 29, 48, 63, 76, 79–83, 146, 189, 193, 199, 201
Roser, Dr., 204
Rozanov, Vasili, 41–2, 44
Russia, 6, 39, 181, 187
Ryan, Dr., 202

SAC (Strategic Air Command) planes, 23, 68, 103, 128–31, 158
St. Anselm, 15–17, 24–5, 31, 34, 166
St. Anthony's Hospital, 203
Saint-Antonin, 94, 141
St. Augustine, 11–12
St. Benedict's field, 3
St. Bernard, 5, 15, 32
St. Brendan, 64
St. Columba, 62
St. Edmund's field, 26
St. Francis, 156
St. Ignatius of Antioch, 164
St. Irenaeus, 206
St. Jerome, 15
St. Joseph's Infirmary, 47
St. Leonard of Port Maurice, 152
St. Malachy's field, 18
St. Maximus, 119
St. Paul, 23, 38
St. Peter's, 81
St. Thomas Aquinas, 110
Salt River, 34, 150
San Blas Islands, 4
Santo Domingo, 180, 187
Sapiential Books, 184
Sartre, Jean-Paul, 10, 20–2, 29, 40, 59
Schachter, Zalman, 51
Scheen, Dr., 87, 151
Schlier, Heinrich, 35–6
Schmitt, F. S., Fr. 15, 34
Seasons of Celebration, 26, 78, 204

Second Epode, 145
Seeds of Destruction, 29, 52, 54, 64, 101, 162, 168
Selma, 163
Shakers, 22, 181
Shakertown, 181
Shan Tung, 205
Shepherdsville, 34
Sign of Jonas, The, xi
Signes, 14, 16
Simon, Dr., 79–80
Six Existentialist Thinkers, 5
Smith, Stevie, 76, 109
Snowmass, 46–8, 189
Sousa, John Philip, 108
South (U.S.), 59, 74, 101, 164, 176–7; *see also places in*
South Africa, 155
South America, 28, 33, 38, 158, 160
Southern Baptist Seminary, 97
Spellman, Cardinal Francis, 11
Spencer, 85, 189; Abbot of, 87–8
Spirit of Simplicity, The, 72
Stanleyville, Congo, 126
Steere, Douglas, 45, 147, 155
Stern, Karl, 194
Stone, Naomi Burton, 141
Story of My Life, 39
Stringfellow, Bill, 68
Study of Good, 158, 169
Sueñens, Cardinal, 79
Suzuki, Dr. Daisetz T., xi, 54–7, 119, 145, 150, 158, 160
Sze, Mai-Mai, 189

Tadié, Marie, 41
Tao of Painting, The, 189
Tarcisius, Father, 80
Teilhard de Chardin, Pierre, 100, 156, 194–5
Tertullian, 176
Tobin, Sister Mary Luke, 79, 113, 135, 182
Tongs of Jeopardy, The, 133–4
Torres, García, 143
Trevor, Meriol, 74, 133, 186
Tshombe, Moise Kapenda, 126
"Two Anti-Poets," 138
Tzu, Chuang, 26, 138, 185, 186

United Nations, 200

Van der Meer, Dom Pierre, 179
Van Doren, Mark, 141
Van Gogh, Vincent, 57, 61
Varela, Blanca, 120
Varieties of Unbelief, 107
Vatican Council, x, 9, 12, 51, 63, 76–7, 79, 81–2, 86, 91, 95, 104, 113, 116, 126, 135, 152, 182
Vatican Pavilion film, 11–12, 14, 21
Vie Spirituelle, La, 145, 150
Vietnam, 70, 111–12, 126, 146, 158, 161, 170, 178, 181, 183, 186, 200, 202–3
Vineyard Knob, 12, 55, 160
Vision of God, The, 116
Voillaume, René, 45
Vousnaya, Youssef, 190
Voyage of St. Brendan, 64–6, 68, 70

Walsh, Dan, 34, 107, 160, 166–7
Walsh, Tony, 100
Warren Commission, 178
Washington, D.C., 42, 178, 181, 185
Weil, Simone, 156–60
"Whistler and His Dog, The," 108–9
Who Is Man, 63
Wilder, A. N., 30
Wilke, Ulfert, 68, 73, 89
Willebrands, Monsignor, 63
Winandy, Dom, 148
Winser, Andrew, 193
Winser, Ann, 193–4
Winzen, Dom Damasus, 148
Woolwich, Bishop of, 58, 66
Word and Revelation, 87
Wright, Bishop, 9
Wu, John, 119, 125, 185, 192, 205
Wygal, Jim, 141, 187, 204

Xavier University, 145

Yamada, Nobozu, 50
Yoder, John Howard, 100–1
Youngstown, Ohio, 138

Zahn, Gordon, 97–8, 145
Zen, 3, 22, 54–7, 62, 82, 89, 106, 119–20, 133, 176, 190, 192, 205